Designing for Accessibility — *an introductory guide*

Contents

Introduction

Designing for Accessibility is an introductory guide to the design of buildings accessible to a wide range of users including people with mobility or sensory impairments, those encumbered with luggage or shopping, parents with young children and older people. With over six million adults in Britain with some degree of disability and an increasing elderly population it becomes ever more important that buildings, whether offices, shops, cinemas, museums, benefit offices, doctors' surgeries, bus stations, church halls or swimming pools, are designed for optimum ease of use by their occupants and visitors.

This guide is based on the belief that the needs of people with disabilities, older people and carers of young children should be considered as an integral part of the design process and that by meeting these needs buildings will perform better for all users. People are complex and their needs cannot simply be itemised in a check-list; for this reason it is important to read and learn from the entire publication rather than by selecting single sections out of context. You will get the most out of this guide by reading it in its entirety before choosing the information most relevant to your own particular interest. This approach may also reveal areas of consideration that you had not previously identified.

In England and Wales the construction of new buildings and the refurbishment of existing ones is governed by the Building Regulations. These regulations comprise a series of requirements covering structure, fire safety, site preparation, toxic substances, thermal and sound insulation, ventilation, hygiene, drainage, heat producing appliances, stairs, ramps and guards, glazing and access for disabled people. A requirement for access was first introduced in August 1985. At the end of 1987 it was replaced by a more detailed requirement and most recently, in June 1992, this was superseded by the latest version. This requirement, Part M of the Building Regulations 1991, requires access for disabled people to all floors of new non-domestic buildings and the provision of facilities such as accessible WCs and spectator seating. Disabled people are defined by Part M as those with mobility impairments or impaired hearing or sight. The original access requirement in 1985 limited the definition to those with mobility impairments and covered only offices, shops and single storey public buildings.

In the eight years that an access requirement has been in force the Centre for Accessible Environments has seen a considerable change for the better in the understanding of what disabled people need from a building and an increased willingness in all but the most narrow-minded to incorporate access into new developments. Now, in 1993, the Department of the Environment, which is responsible for devising the Building Regulations, is considering extending the access requirement to major alterations of existing buildings.

Access for disabled building users is clearly a subject to be taken seriously. This guide attempts to introduce those unfamiliar with the subject to a basic understanding of what accessibility entails. It does not attempt to replace Part M of the Building Regulations and readers engaged in work which falls within the scope of Part M are advised to obtain a copy of *Approved Document M* to read in conjunction with this guide. The main part of the booklet covers the basic design considerations, the appendices cover the importance of building management in ensuring the continuance of an accessible environment, fire safety, relevant legislation, useful organisations and trade associations and further reading.

Readers of *Designing for Accessibility* who have questions to ask about its content or about work on which they are engaged are invited to contact the Centre for Accessible Environments for information and advice. Full details of the Centre and the services it offers are given in appendix four.

Car parking

Larger parking bays are required to allow people with reduced mobility to get into and out of their cars with the minimum of difficulty.

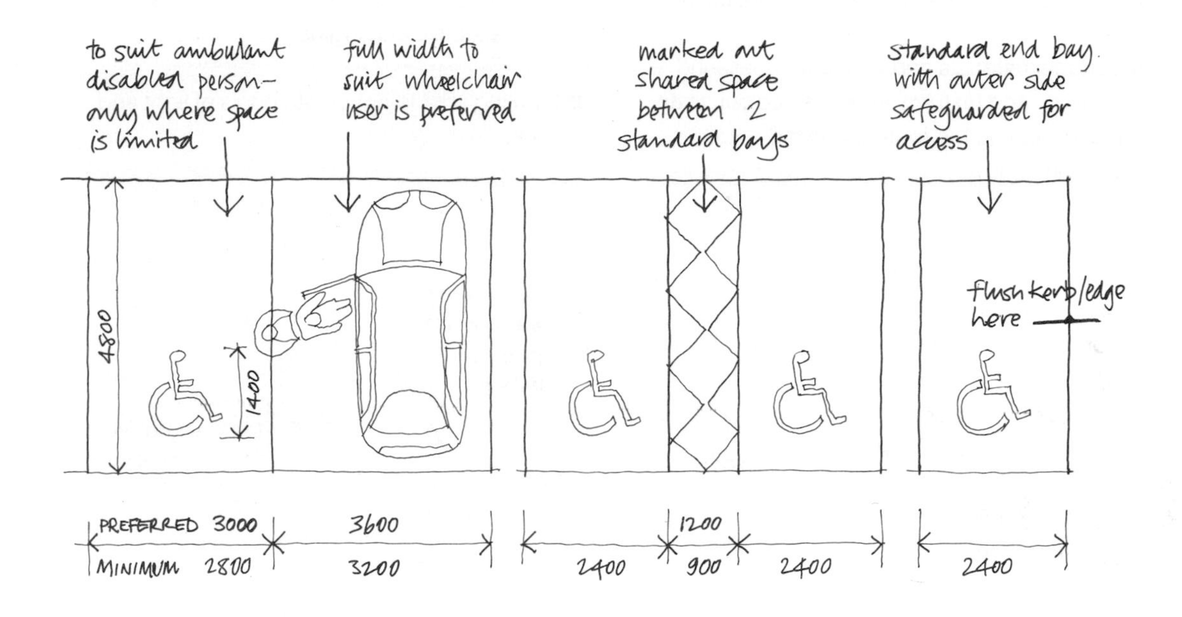

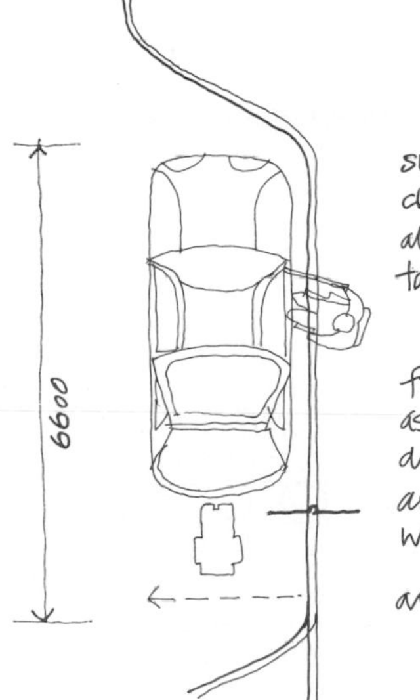

- The location of accessible bays should be clearly signposted from the car park entrance.
- Bays should be identified as provision for disabled drivers or passengers only.
- Bays should be close to the facilities the car park serves — within 50m if uncovered, 100m covered.
- Bays need to be wide enough to allow car doors to be fully opened to allow disabled drivers and passengers to transfer to a wheelchair parked alongside.
- Kerbs between the parking area and routes to buildings should be dropped to give access to wheelchair users.
- The car park surface should be smooth and even and free from loose stones.

Routes

Routes should provide ample aural and tactile information as well as visual clues to help people with sight impairments.

- Landmarks are helpful for orientation and as well as providing visual clues can incorporate audible ones such as fountains.
- Surface materials can offer different sound qualities and textures as well as colour as an aid to locating the route within the environment.
- Planting can provide scent and colour.
- Signs should be carefully located, clear, non-reflective and logical.
- Lighting should not create pools of light and dark.

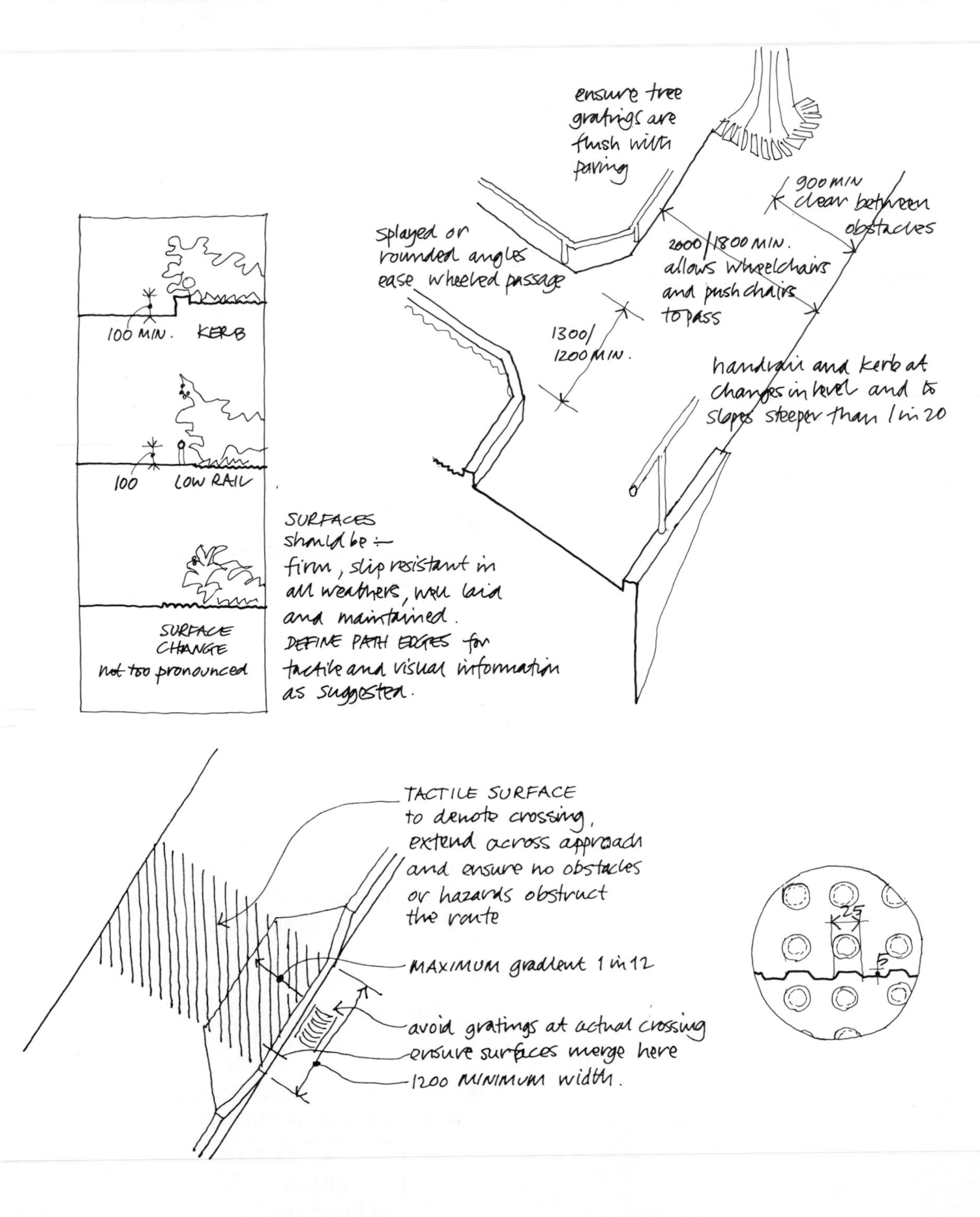

Street furniture

Carelessly placed street furniture causes problems for people with sight impairments and obstructs the passage of wheelchair users.

- The provision of appropriate seating is important for people with disabilities.

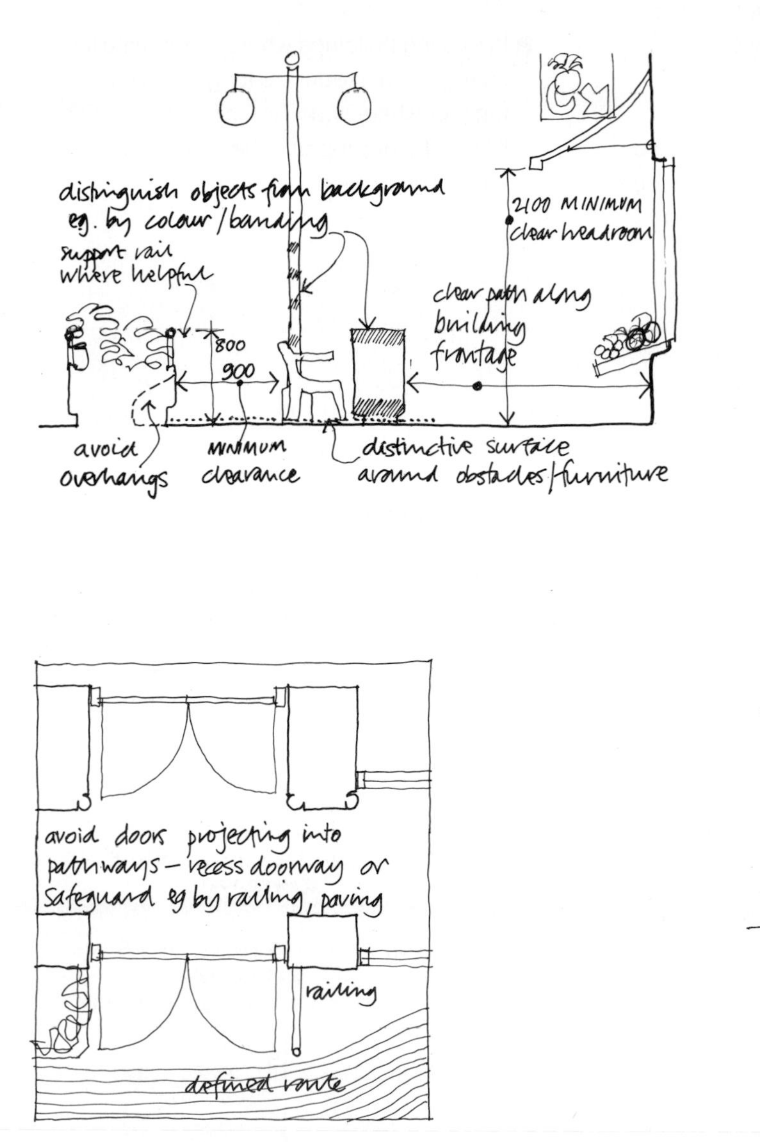

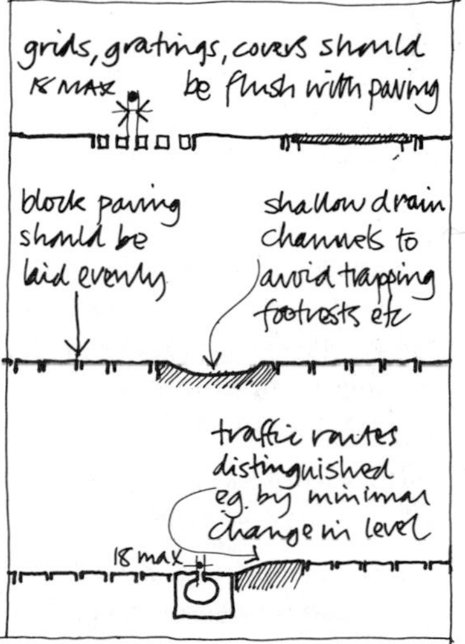

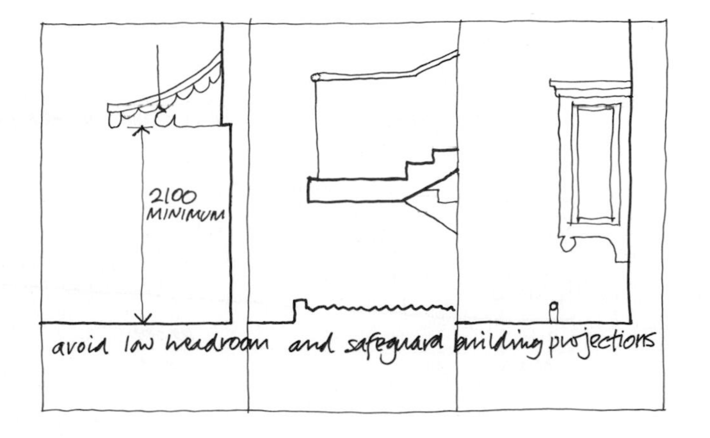

Ramps

Ramps are essential to enable wheelchair users and parents with pushchairs to overcome level changes, but ideally they should be accompanied by steps for ambulant disabled people.

- A gradient of 1:20 is considered 'level'. 1:15 is adequate and 1:12 is the absolute maximum. The steeper the gradient, the shorter the length of ramp between landings.
- Handrails should be provided and formed from materials that are not cold to the touch, for example hardwood or nylon-coated steel.
- The handrail should be easily distinguishable from its background for the benefit of people with sight impairments.
- Surface materials should be slip-resistant, firmly-fixed and easy to maintain.
- In existing buildings where an extreme level change would require a long circuitous ramp or where space is limited a short-rise lift may be appropriate. See the section on vertical circulation.

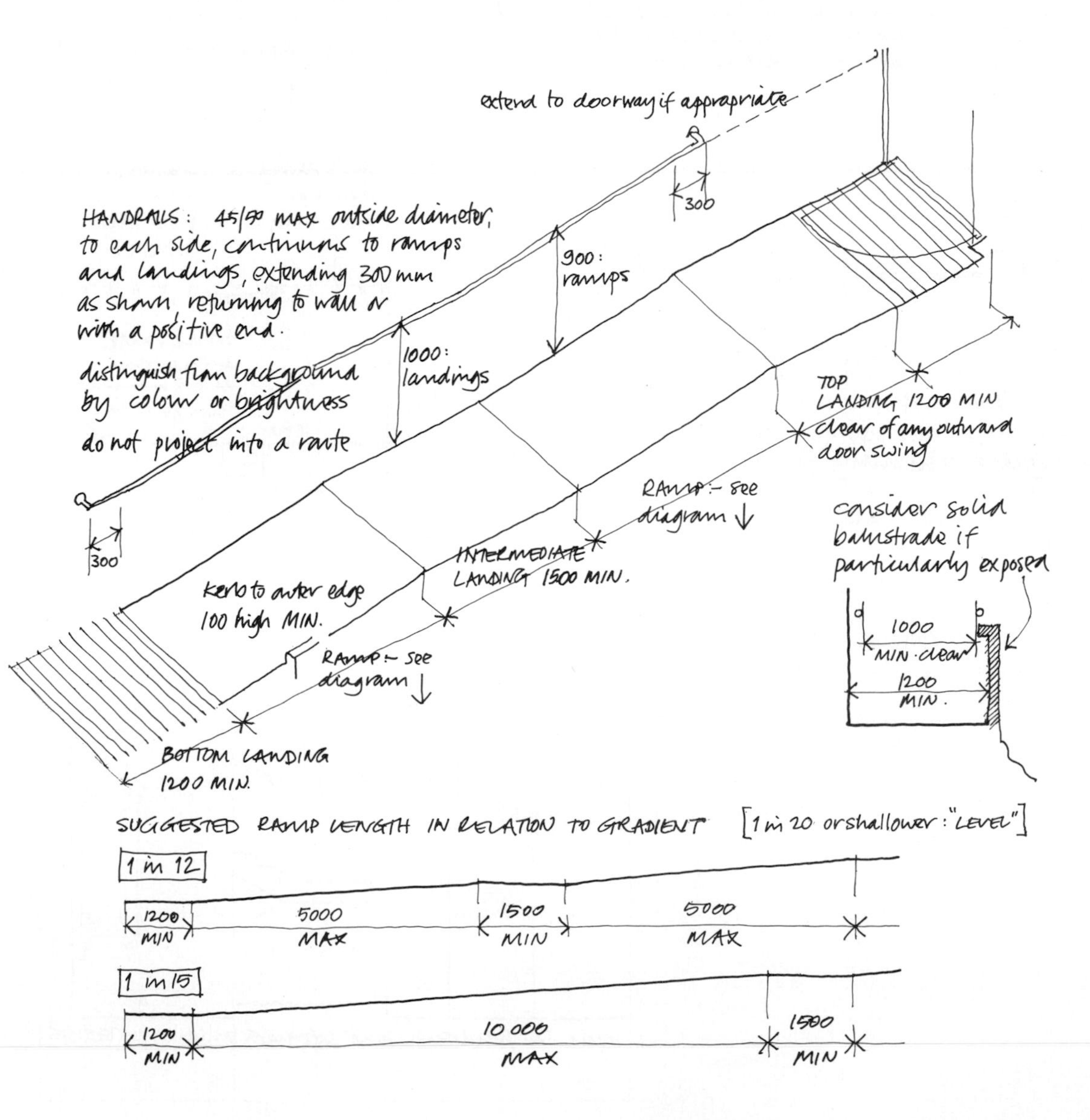

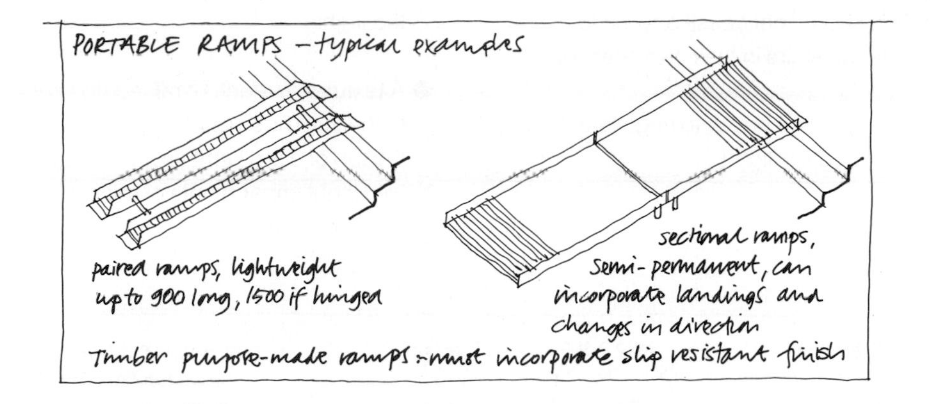

Steps

Steps are preferred to ramps by some ambulant disabled people.

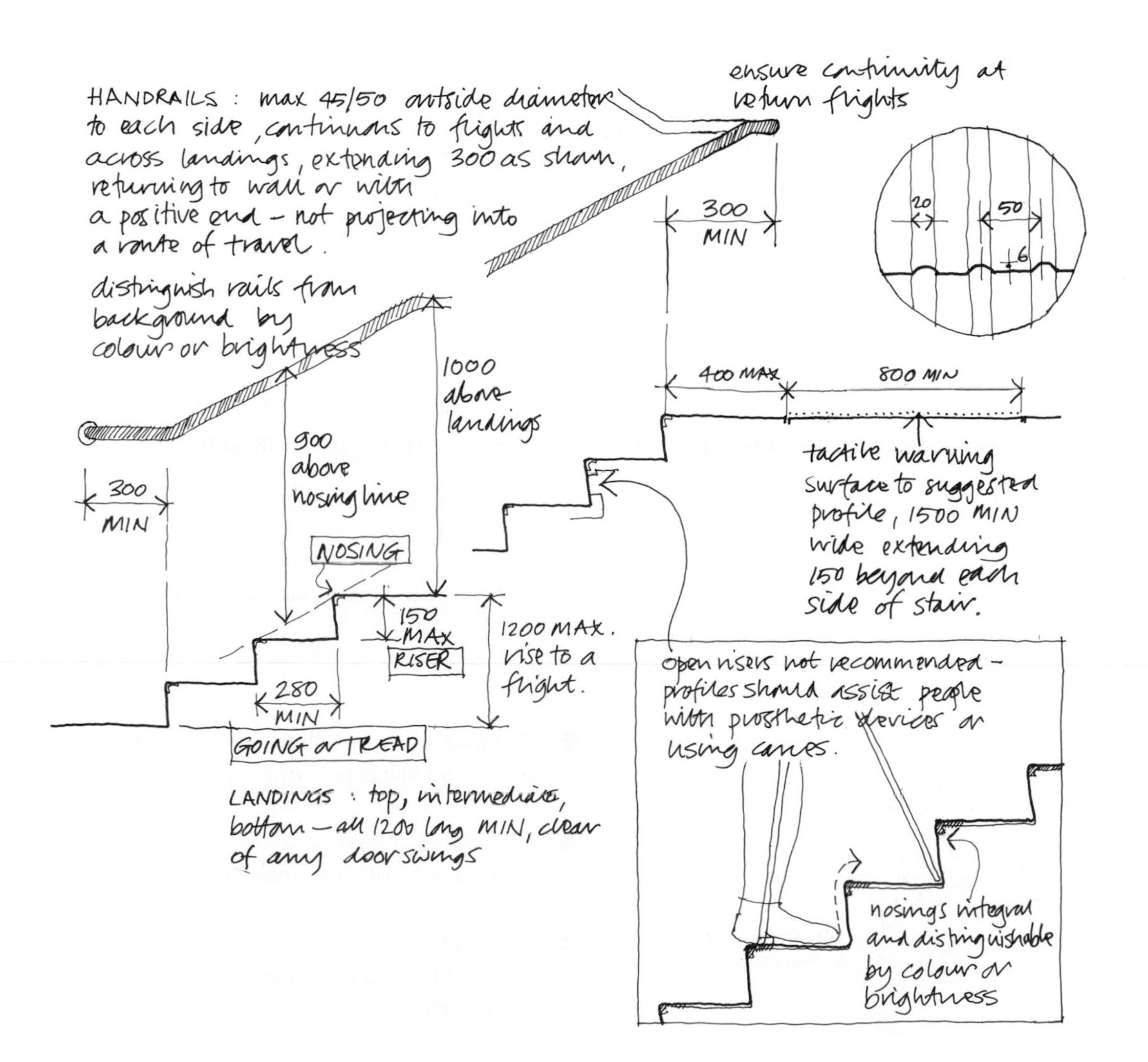

STEPS

- Lighting should be located at the side of the flight and should not cause anyone to negotiate the stairs in their own shadow.
- Straight flights are easier to negotiate than curved or dogleg flights.
- Handrails should be provided however short the flight.
- A textured surface of raised ribs set parallel to the step nosings should be provided at the top of each flight as a warning to people with sight impairments of the presence of a tripping hazard.

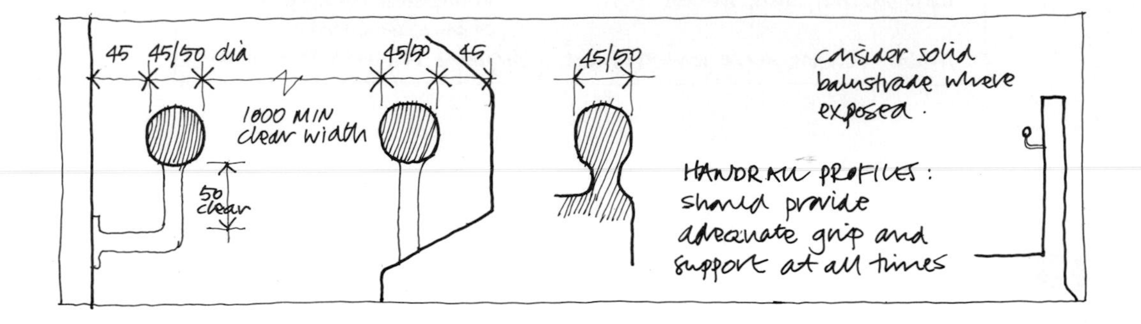

Entrances

Entrances to buildings should be placed in a logical relationship with the routes that serve them and should be easily distinguishable from the facade.

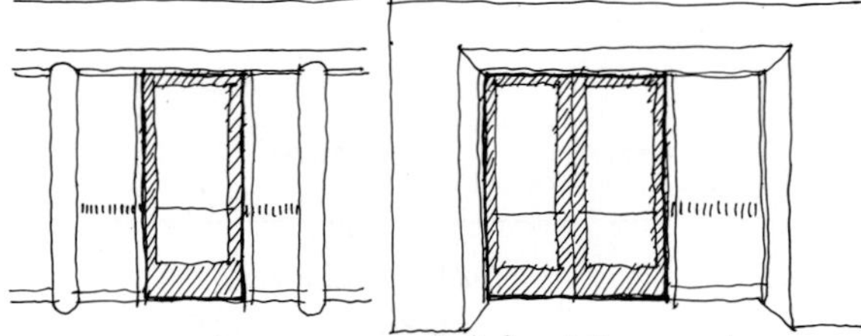

ensure entrances are distinguishable by detailing, colour or other features

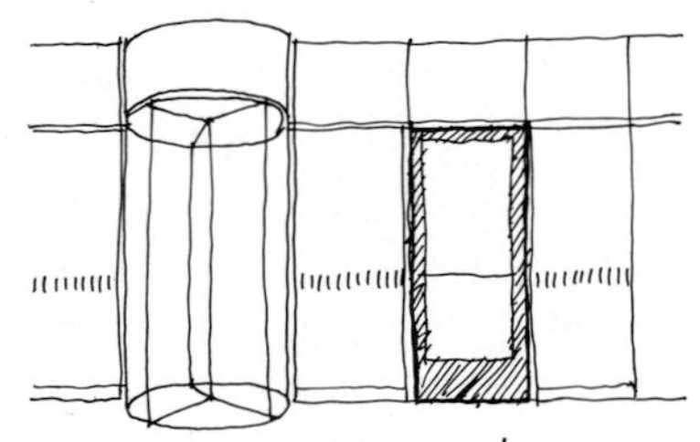

provide accessible entrance adjacent to standard size revolving doors, preferably in common use for entry

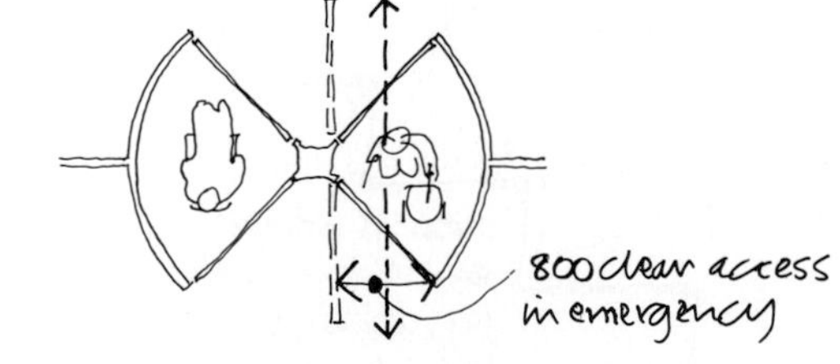

- Substantially glazed entrances must bear markings for safety and visibility.
- Door handles should be selected for ease of grip by people with poor manual dexterity.
- Door closers should be adjusted to the minimum force necessary and should be regularly maintained.
- Thresholds should be flush.

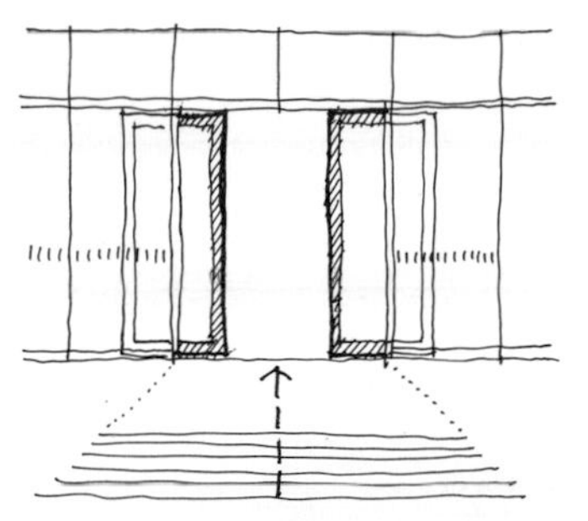

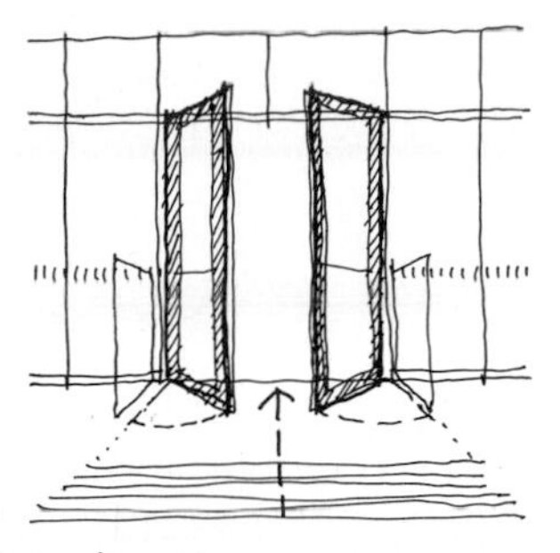

AUTOMATIC OPENING DOORS – define approach, provide tactile and visual information; hinged doors are potentially hazardous – safeguard the immediate approach to them.

- Automatic doors generally offer very good access for disabled people, but those that swing towards the user can be dangerous.
- Automatic doors should remain open long enough for a slow-moving person to pass through.
- Conventional revolving doors should be supplemented by a single leaf, side-hung door that is in regular use.
- Large revolving doors designed to accommodate supermarket trolleys, pushchairs and wheelchairs move automatically at a speed determined by the slowest person using them. It should be noted that despite this some ambulant disabled people, particularly older people, and people with sight impairments may not have the confidence to use them.
- Immediately inside the entrance door there should be a lighting transition zone within the lobby where people with sight impairments are able to adjust from a bright outdoors to a more dimly lit interior.
- Lobbies should be sized to allow wheelchair users to move clear of the first door before negotiating the second.
- Signage should be obvious and clear, indicating where visitors should go to find the reception, information point, lifts, stairs or WCs.

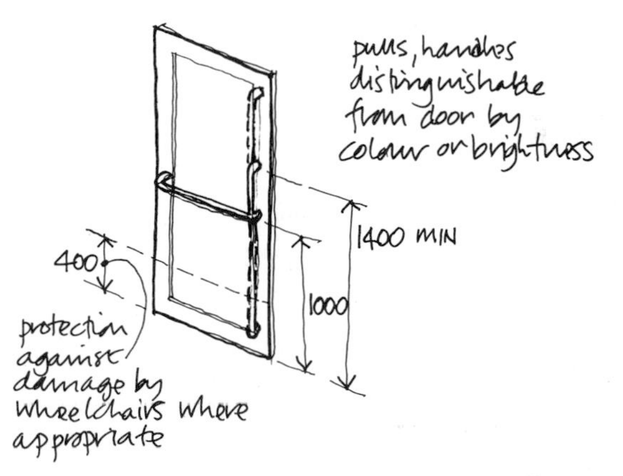

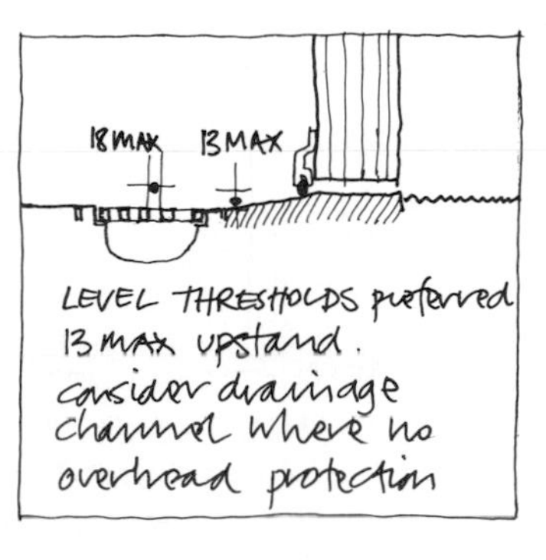

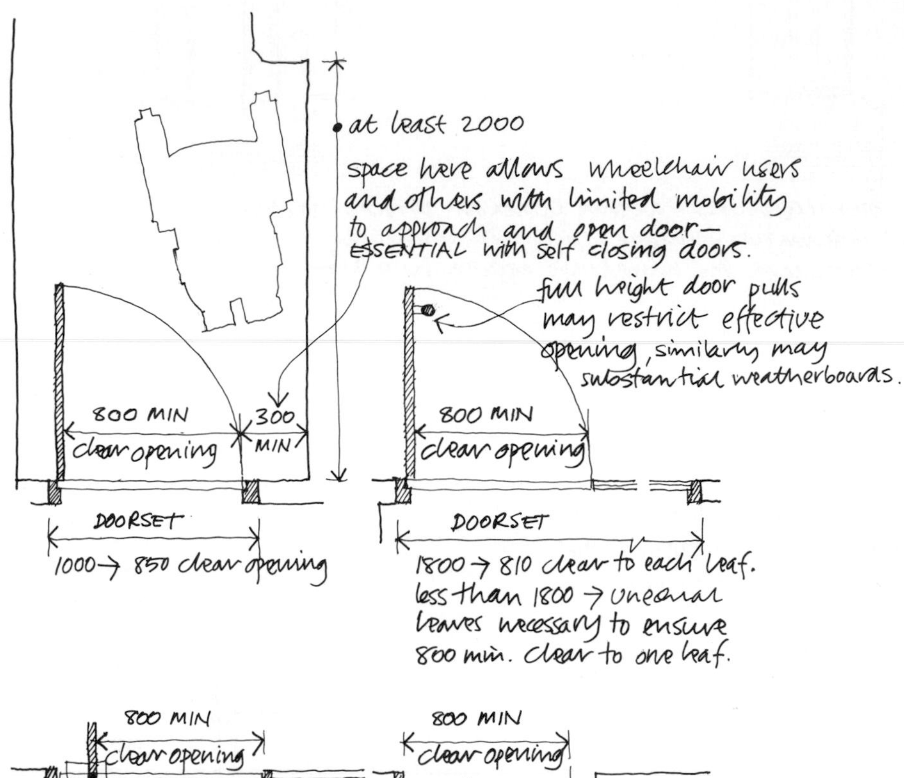

maintain clear opening width with pivotted or sliding doors

EXIT DOORS : where not combined with entrances these also should have clear opening widths as above as well as level thresholds, and external ramps where necessary.

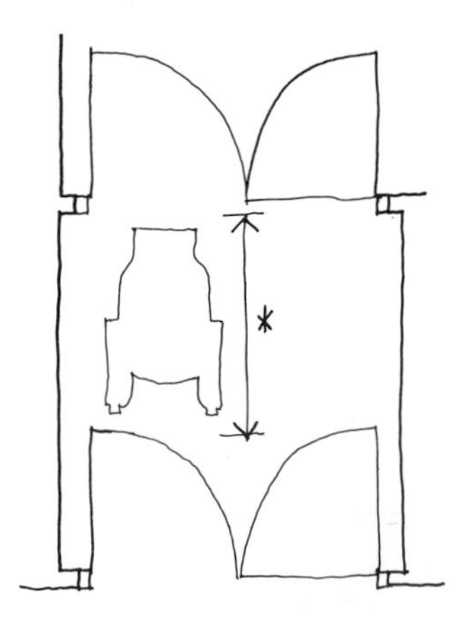

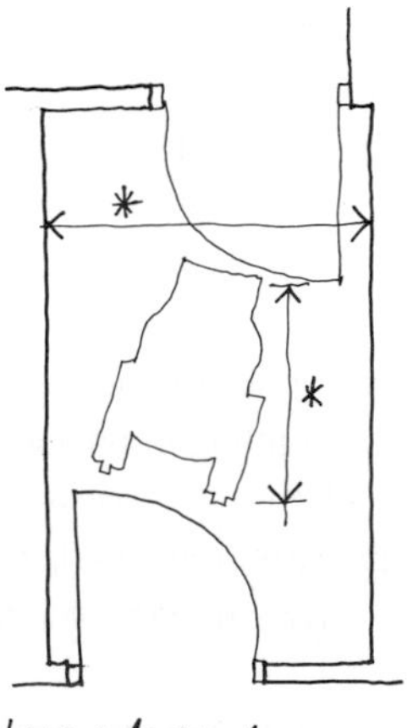

LAYOUT OF LOBBIES : will be determined by door layout and operation and by need of wheelchair users and others to pass clear of one door before approaching and opening the second and preferably with a minimum of manoeuvring

*: critical dimensions

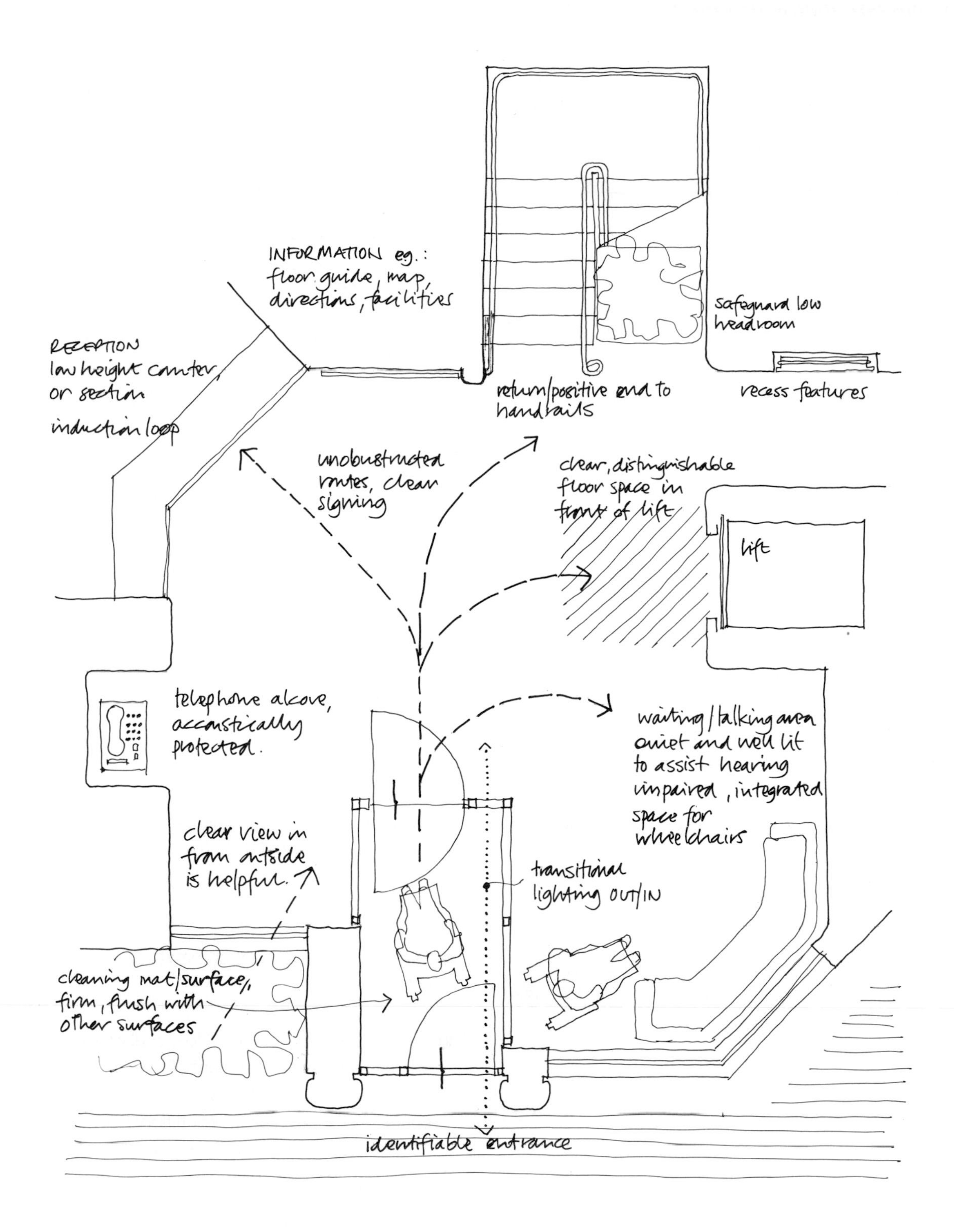
INFORMATION eg.:
floor guide, map,
directions, facilities
RECEPTION
low height counter,
or section
induction loop
return/positive end to
handrails
safeguard low
headroom
recess features
unobstructed
routes, clear
signing
clear, distinguishable
floor space in
front of lift
lift
telephone alcove,
acoustically
protected.
waiting/talking area
quiet and well lit
to assist hearing
impaired, integrated
space for
wheelchairs
clear view in
from outside
is helpful.
transitional
lighting OUT/IN
cleaning mat/surface,
firm, flush with
other surfaces
identifiable entrance

ENTRANCES

Horizontal circulation

Corridors connect spaces and in emergencies form part of escape routes. They must be simple and safe to negotiate. Corridors convey information about a building in order to assist with circulation around it.

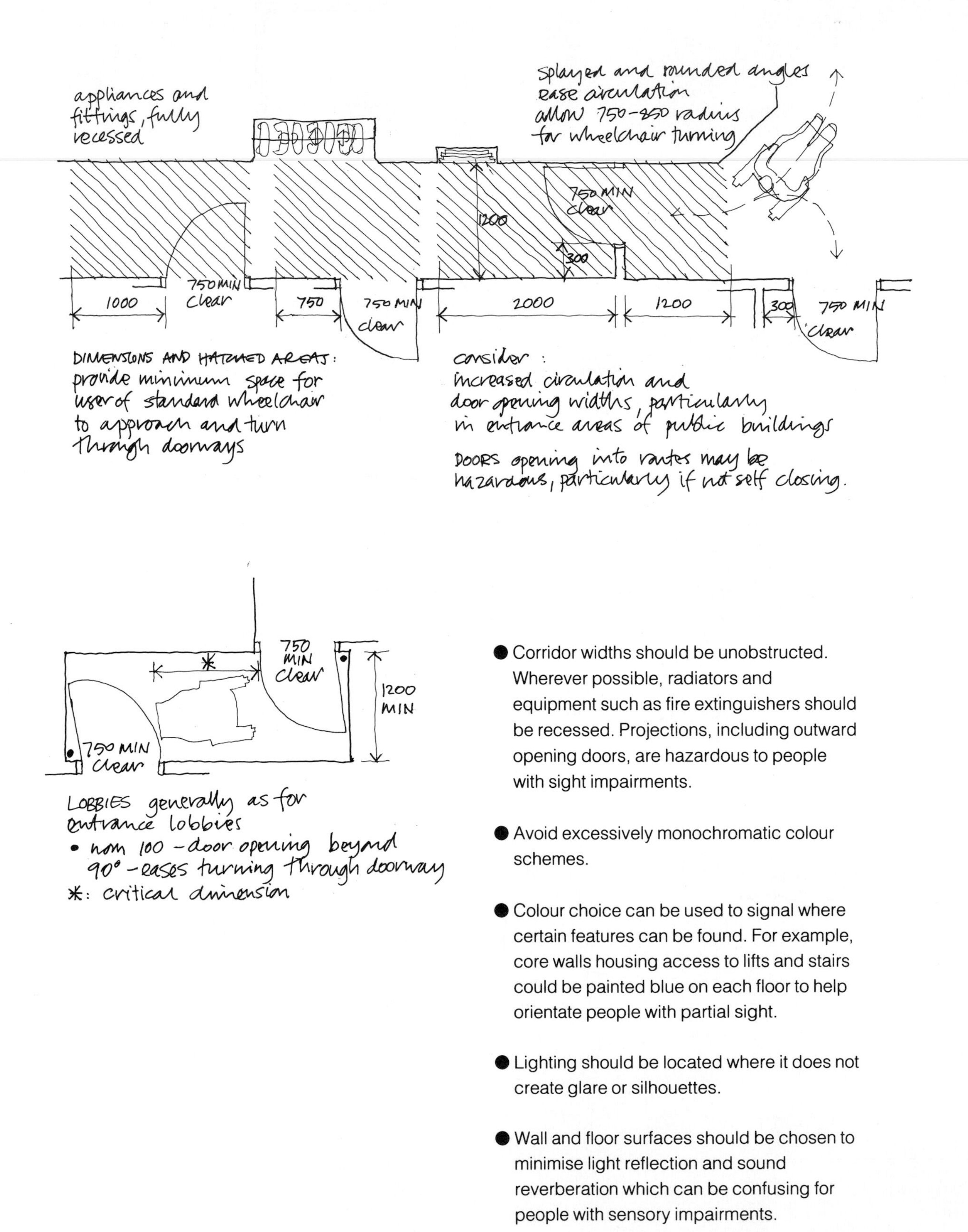

- Corridor widths should be unobstructed. Wherever possible, radiators and equipment such as fire extinguishers should be recessed. Projections, including outward opening doors, are hazardous to people with sight impairments.
- Avoid excessively monochromatic colour schemes.
- Colour choice can be used to signal where certain features can be found. For example, core walls housing access to lifts and stairs could be painted blue on each floor to help orientate people with partial sight.
- Lighting should be located where it does not create glare or silhouettes.
- Wall and floor surfaces should be chosen to minimise light reflection and sound reverberation which can be confusing for people with sensory impairments.

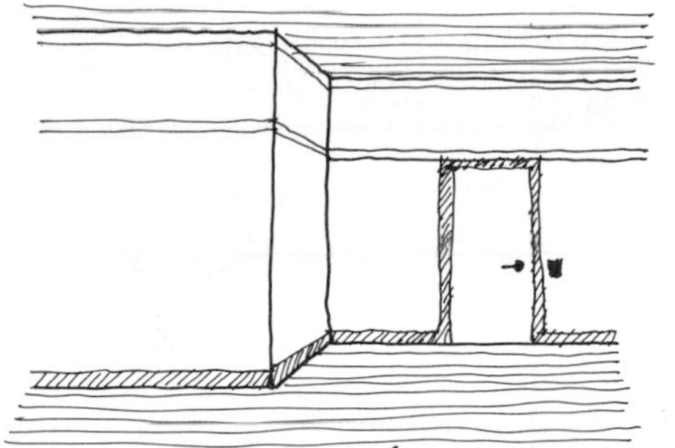

provide visual information by distinguishing floor, wall and ceiling planes, door surrounds, decorative features

Vertical circulation

Lifts are usually the easiest way of travelling between different levels, but stairs, ramps, platform lifts and wheelchair stairlifts may also be used.

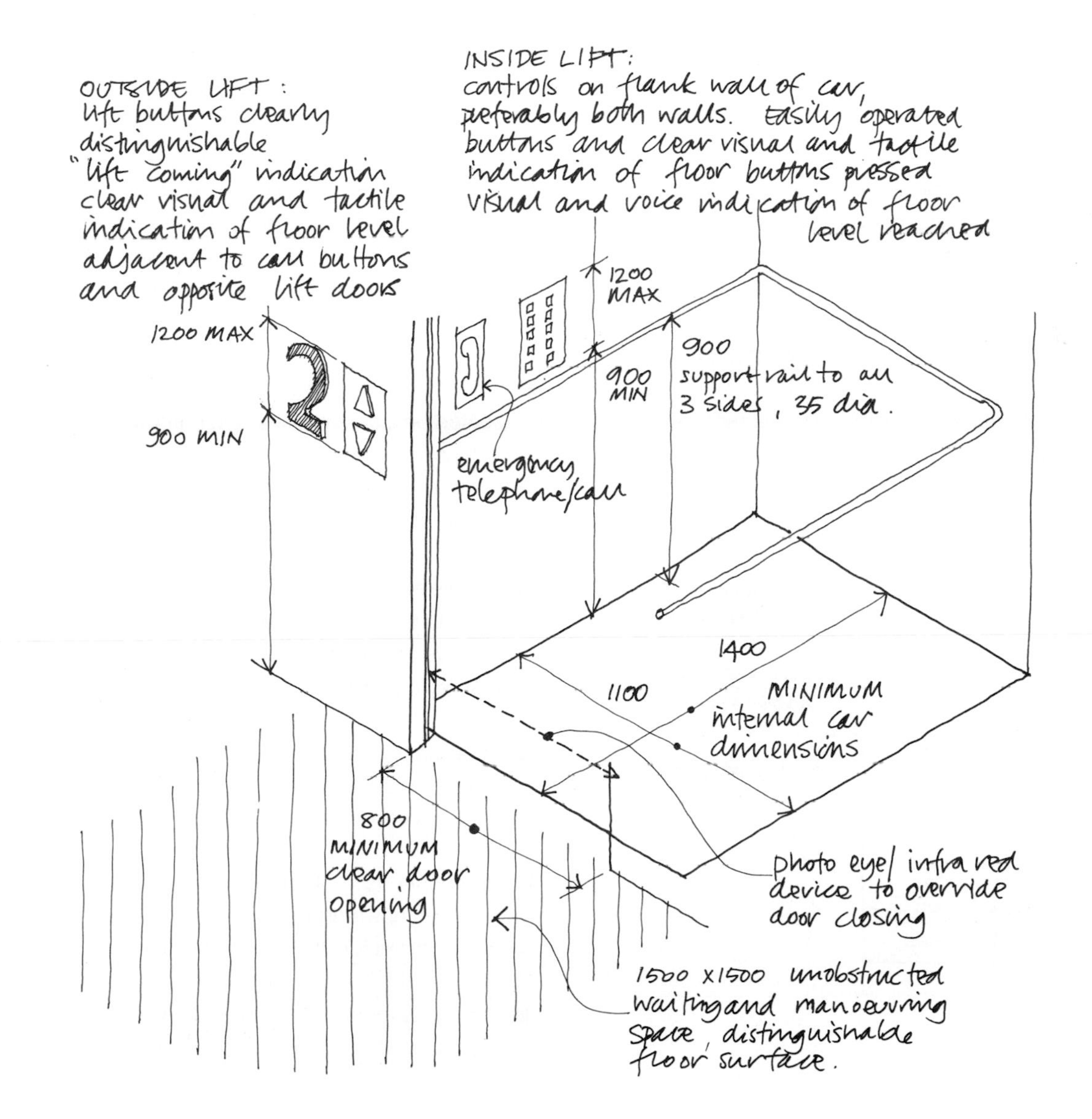

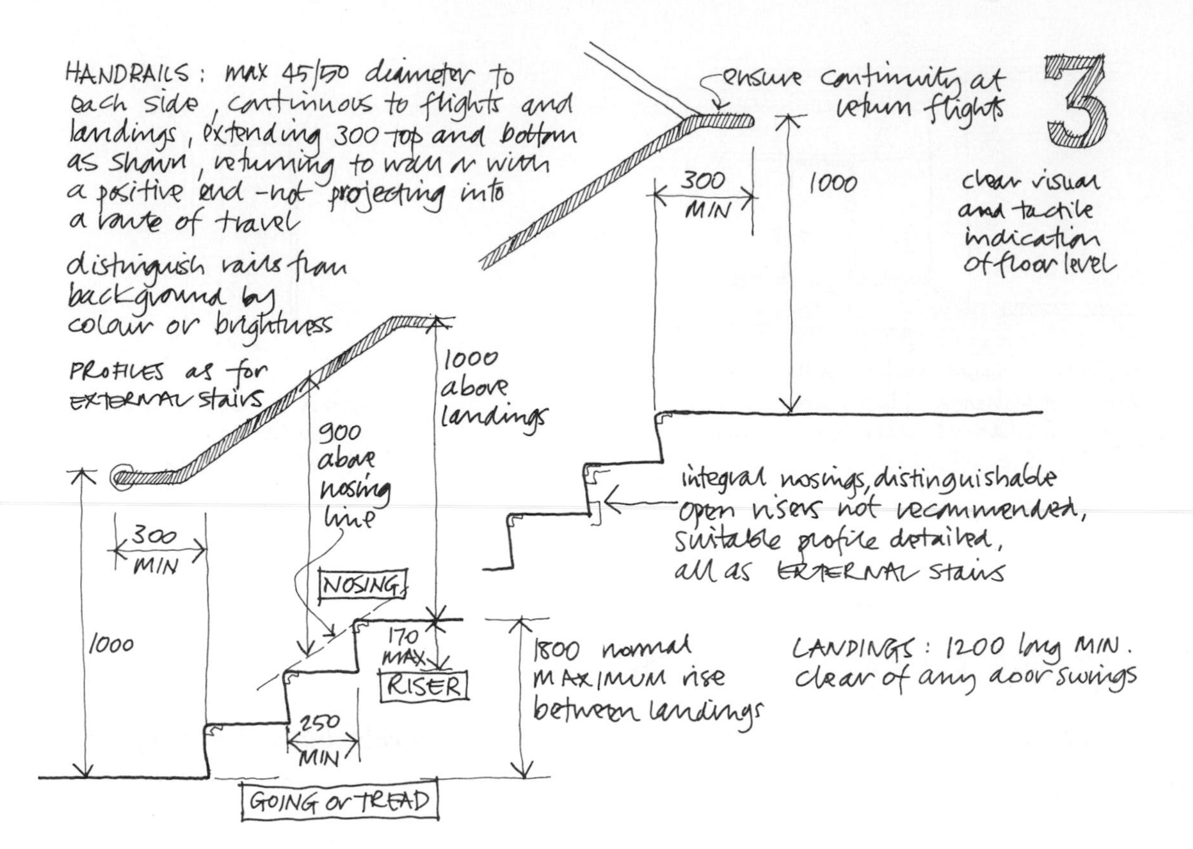

- Lifts should be served by landings large enough for wheelchair users to turn to reverse into the lift.
- The call panel should be easily distinguishable from its background.

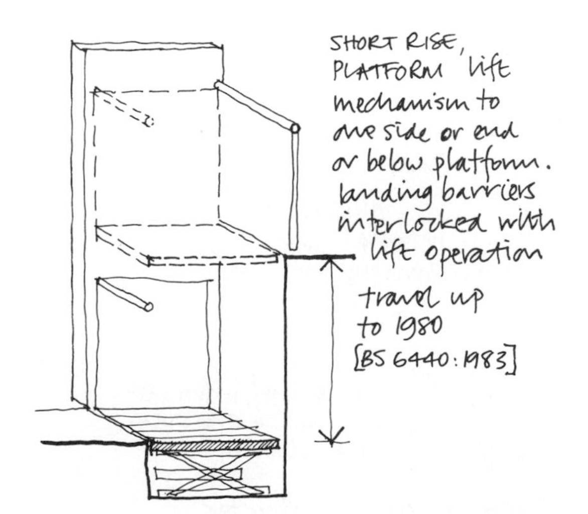

- Lift doors should remain open for an adequate time to allow entry. Door reactivating devices are necessary to ensure no one can get trapped in the lift doors.
- Inside the lift, the control panel should be located on a side wall. Raised numbers on buttons help people with sight impairments; braille is read by only a small proportion of the visually impaired population.
- Audible announcements of the floor reached help people with poor sight; visual displays are necessary for people with hearing impairments.
- Emergency telephones in lifts should contain inductive couplers so that hearing aid users can make use of them.
- Alarm buttons in lifts should be fitted with a visual acknowledgement that the alarm bell has sounded for lift users unable to hear it.
- The points identified in the section on external steps and ramps are relevant here.

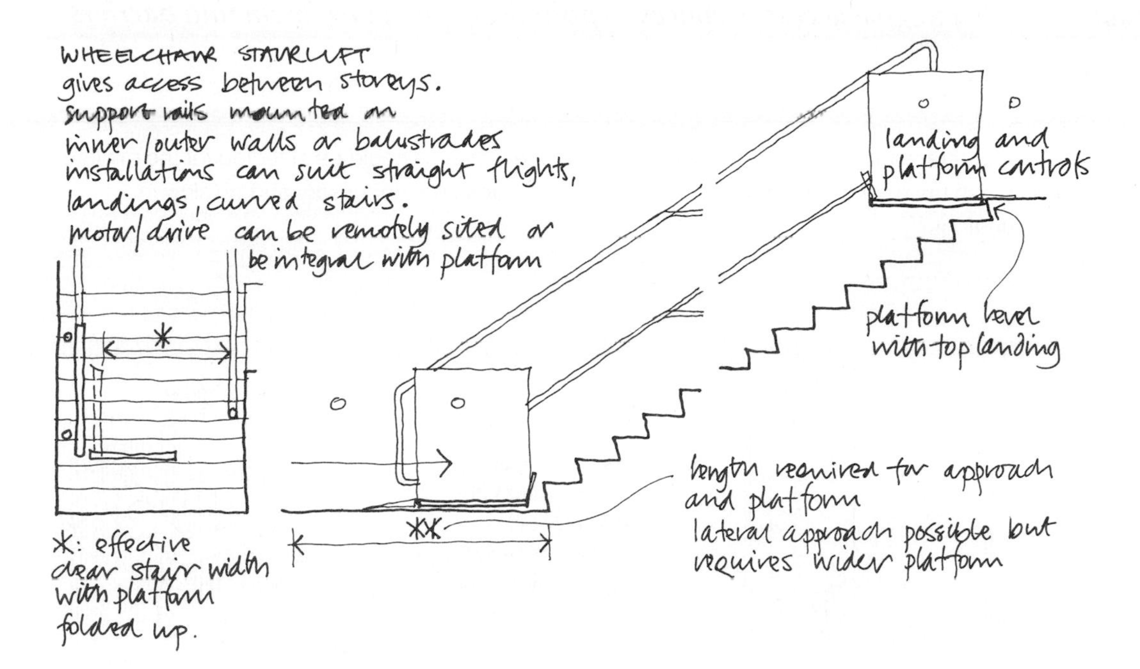

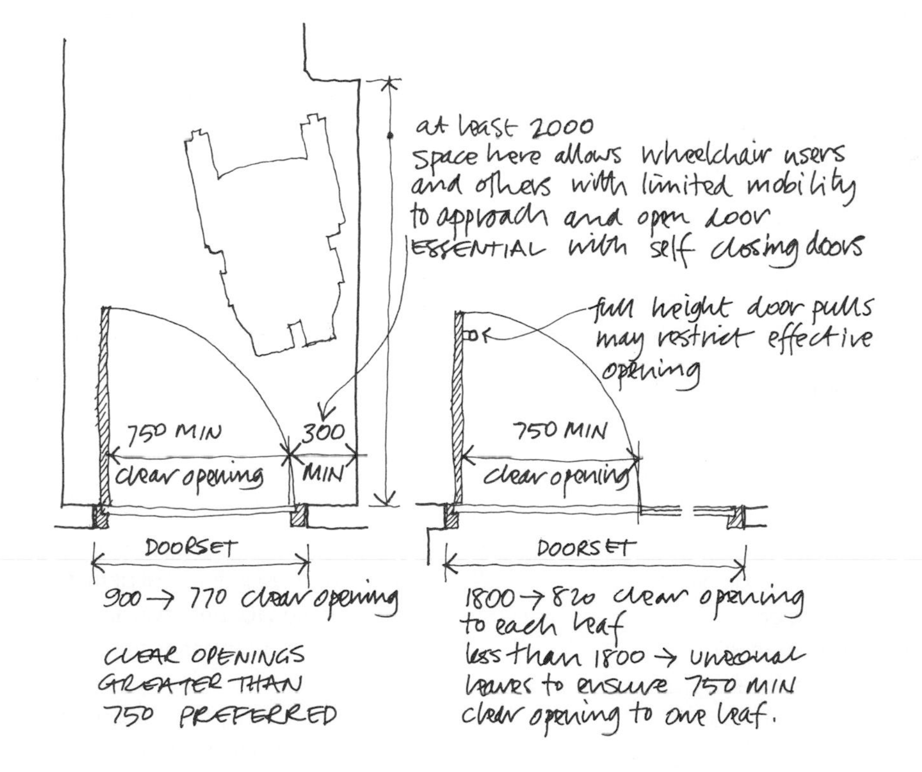

VERTICAL CIRCULATION

Doors

Doors are intended to give access to spaces — poor design will turn them into barriers between spaces.

- Colour contrast should be used to help distinguish the door frame from its surroundings.

- Closers should be selected for the minimum pressure necessary and be slow in operation.

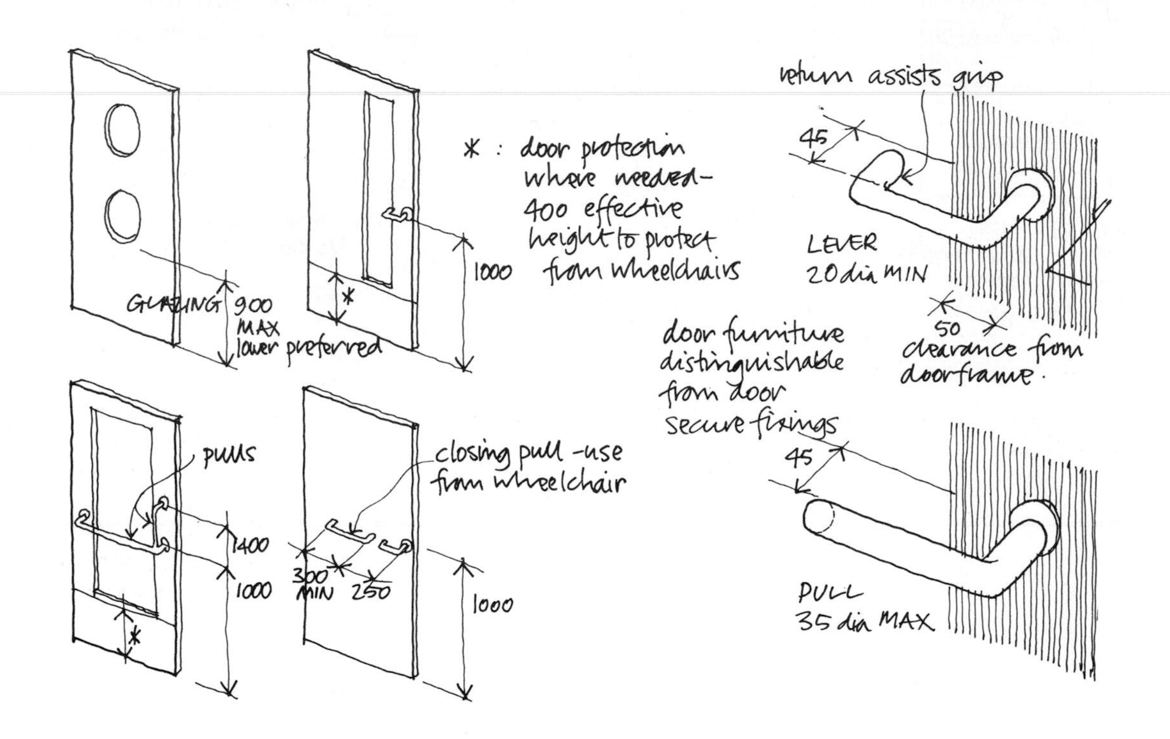

Lavatories

Accessible WCs are essential for the freedom of people with disabilities.

- Wheelchair users commonly use WCs in one of three ways: lateral transfer, angled transfer or frontal use. A small number of wheelchair users may transfer backwards onto the WC with assistance from a helper after removing the back support of their wheelchair.

- The conventional unisex WC can accommodate a variety of methods of transfer and allows most users to wash their hands while seated on the WC before transferring back to their chair.

- The peninsular layout does not permit hand washing from the WC, but does allow for transfer to the WC from either side.

- Ceramic tiles and shiny floors should not cause reflection of fittings or glare from lights as this will confuse people with sight impairments.

- A slip-resistant flooring material in a contrasting colour to the walls is important for safety reasons.

LAYOUT PRINCIPLES

TRANSFER OPTIONS:

A: across from wheelchair on to WC, wheelchair backed or driven up to rear wall – hence need for WC projection

B: angled transfer using rails and/or grasping WC

C: head on transfer using rails to pivot from chair to WC

STANDARD LAYOUT: allows for use of basin and fittings from seated position on WC. Handed layouts recommended where more than 1 accessible lavatory in a building

PENINSULAR LAYOUT: allows for approach and transfer from either side but not for use of basin from WC

Hand outward opening door to suit approach, space at * helpful, min 100, if handing as shown

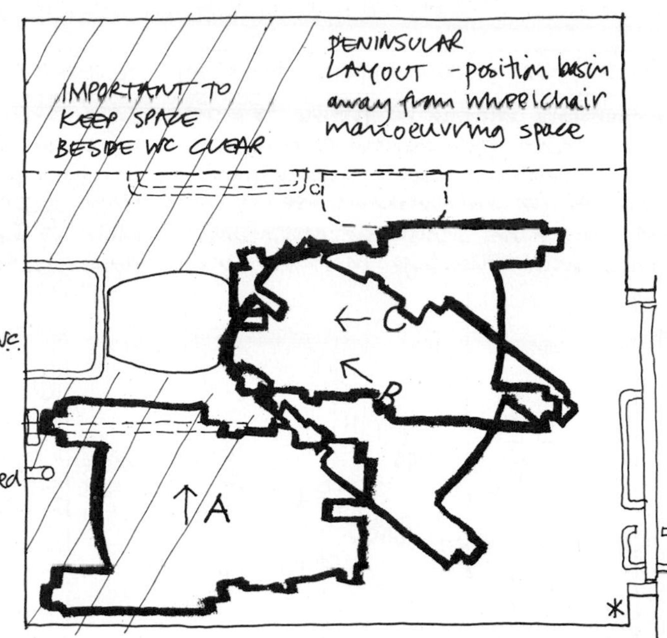

MINIMUM DIMENSIONS

STANDARD – 1500 W x 2000 L
PENINSULAR – 2500 W x 2000 L
increase these where possible

DOOR: conventionally opens outwards. may with advantage open in provided there is space clear of doorswing and fittings of 700 x 1100 MINIMUM and door can be opened outwards in emergency

1400
700
450
400 approx
500 MIN
800
200
1500

DOOR may open inwards provided clear space is maintained and emergency outward opening detailed.

- The colour or tone of the background should allow for easy distinguishability of grab rails and sanitary fittings.

- The WC layout for ambulant disabled people could usefully be adopted as a universal model as it allows space for entry to the cubicle with a child or with shopping.

- Where several unisex or ambulant WCs are provided the opportunity should be taken to hand the layouts.

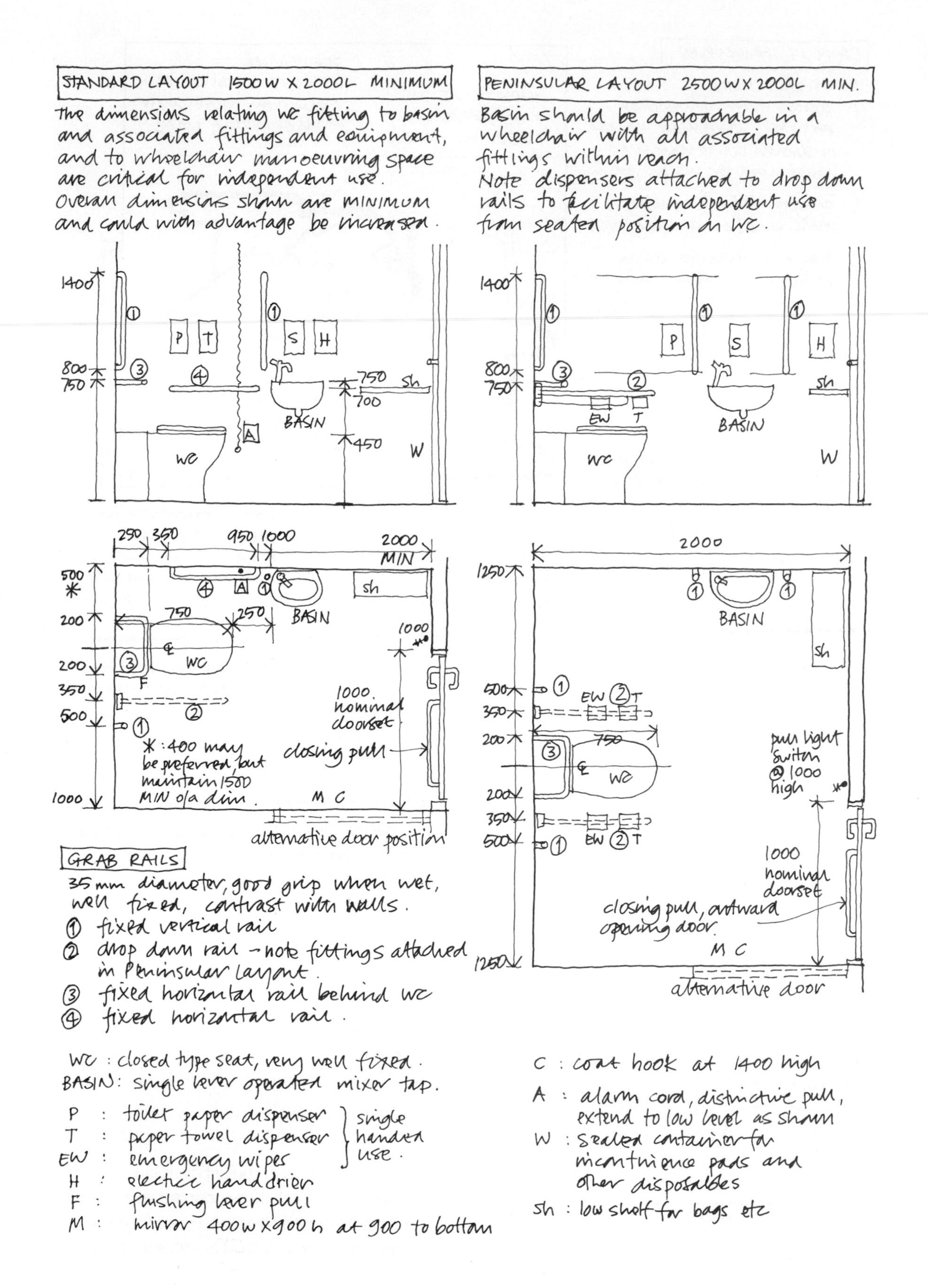
STANDARD LAYOUT 1500W X 2000L MINIMUM
The dimensions relating WC fitting to basin and associated fittings and equipment, and to wheelchair manoeuvring space are critical for independent use. Overall dimensions shown are MINIMUM and could with advantage be increased.
PENINSULAR LAYOUT 2500W X 2000L MIN.
Basin should be approachable in a wheelchair with all associated fittings within reach.
Note dispensers attached to drop down rails to facilitate independent use from seated position on WC.
1400
800
750
P
T
S
H
BASIN
WC
W
A
EW
sh
750
700
450
250
350
950
1000
2000 MIN
500 *
200
200
350
500
1000
F
1000 nominal doorset
closing pull
* : 400 may be preferred, but maintain 1500 MIN o/a dim.
M C
alternative door position
2000
1250
pull light switch @ 1000 high
closing pull, outward opening door.
alternative door
GRAB RAILS
35mm diameter, good grip when wet, well fixed, contrast with walls.
① fixed vertical rail
② drop down rail – note fittings attached in Peninsular layout.
③ fixed horizontal rail behind WC
④ fixed horizontal rail.
WC : closed type seat, very well fixed.
BASIN : single lever operated mixer tap.
P : toilet paper dispenser
T : paper towel dispenser
EW : emergency wipes
single handed use.
H : electric hand drier
F : flushing lever pull
M : mirror 400w x 900h at 900 to bottom
C : coat hook at 1400 high
A : alarm cord, distinctive pull, extend to low level as shown
W : sealed container for incontinence pads and other disposables
sh : low shelf for bags etc

LAVATORIES

Fixtures, fittings and services

Seating

- Seats should be provided at intervals along long routes (both internal and external) or where waiting is likely.
- Seats should be stable and offered in a range of heights.
- If seats are recessed there should be space for a wheelchair user to pull up alongside a seated companion.

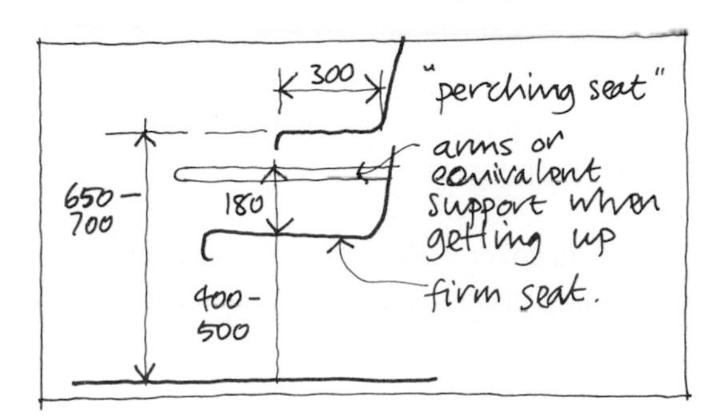

Counters and checkouts

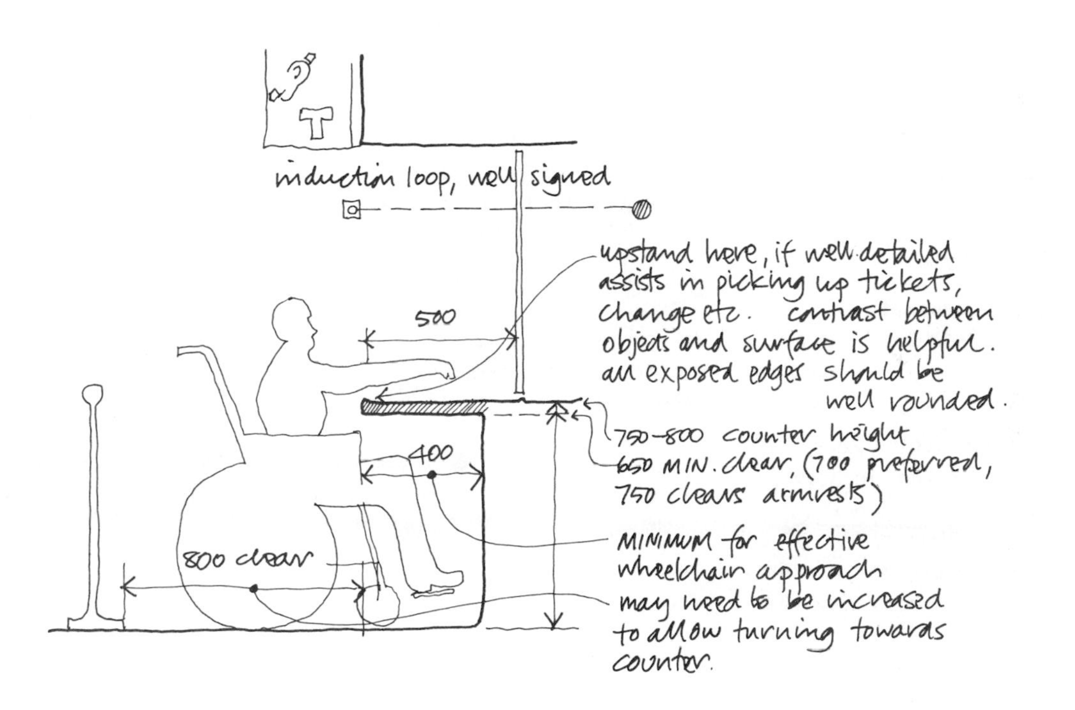

- All, or some, counters and checkouts should be wide enough for wheelchair users and parents with pushchairs.
- Induction loops fitted at counters will help people with hearing aids.
- Lighting at glazed counters should not cause reflections which reduce a person's ability to lip-read.

Telephones

● Inductive couplers should be fitted to all telephones to enable people with hearing aids to use them.

● Telephones should be fixed at a height that allows wheelchair users to read any visual display panels.

● Where several telephones are provided a range of fixing heights to suit standing and seated users could be adopted.

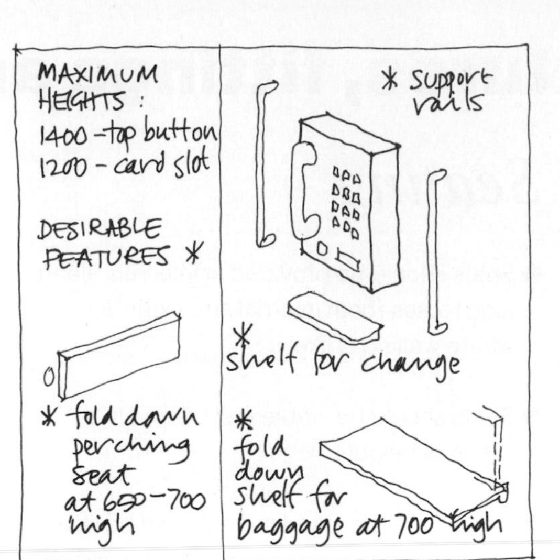

Automatic teller machines

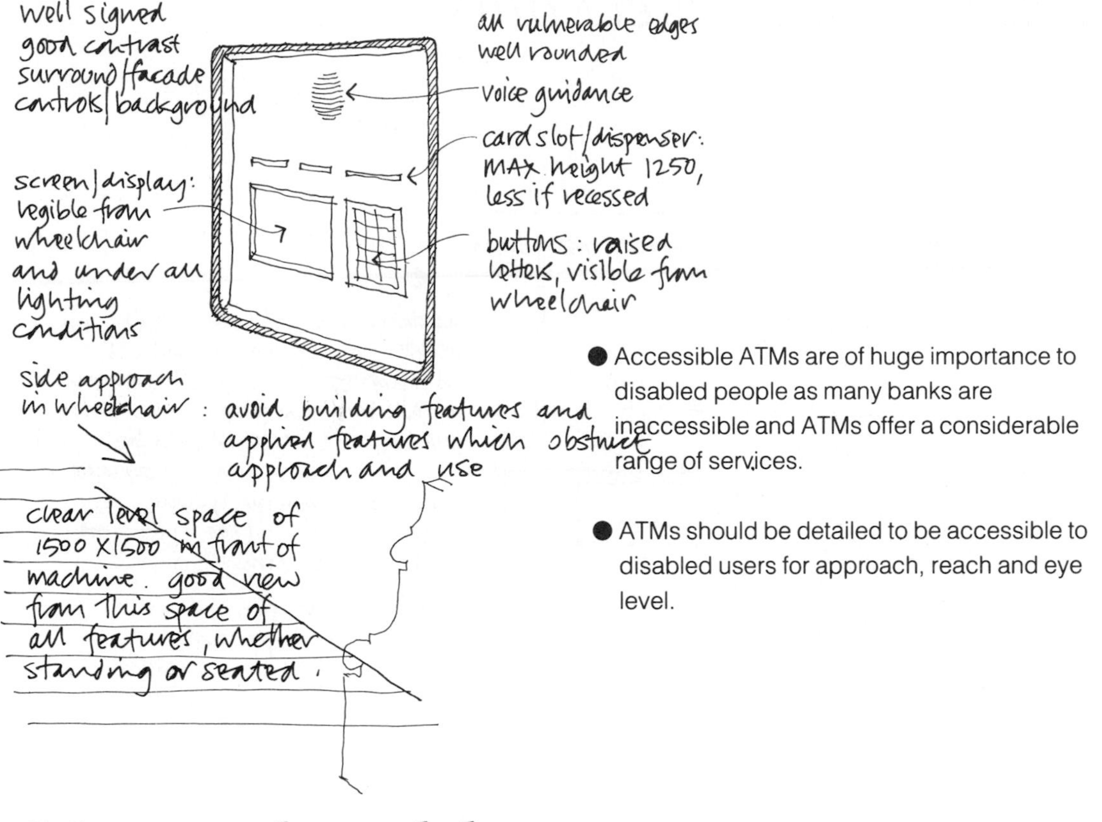

● Accessible ATMs are of huge importance to disabled people as many banks are inaccessible and ATMs offer a considerable range of services.

● ATMs should be detailed to be accessible to disabled users for approach, reach and eye level.

Maps and models

● Maps can usefully supplement signs. They help people with hearing impairments who may not be able to ask for or understand verbal directions.

● Tactile maps benefit people with sight impairments who may be unable to read signs.

● Models of the interior layout of public buildings, particularly those of architectural interest, aid the comprehension of the building by people with sight impairments.

● Where a building relies upon its own vocabulary of textured surfaces to convey information to people with sight impairments a key must be offered at a central information point.

Signs

- Signs should be clear, legible and obvious.
- Signs provide reassurance as well as information. Care should be taken to ensure that signage gaps do not appear along a route to a facility.
- Written signs should be in a mixture of upper and lower case as words are recognised by shape not individual letters.
- Letters, numbers and pictograms should contrast in colour and tone with the background of the sign.
- Embossed letters, raised pictograms and direction arrows help people with sight impairments.

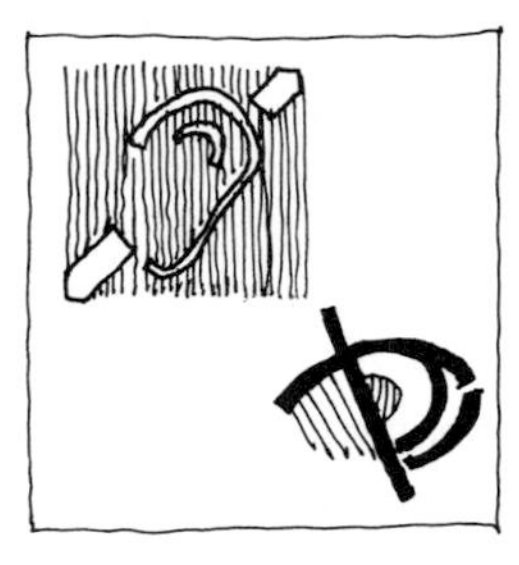

Induction loops and infrared systems

- Induction loops work by converting sound via a microphone into a varying magnetic field which is converted back to amplified sound by an individual's hearing aid. Loops help to cut out extraneous background noise.
- Induction loops should be fitted wherever information is given verbally: airports, railway stations, box offices, ticket counters, banks, post offices, churches, meeting rooms, cinemas and theatres. Induction loops do allow sound to be picked up by hearing aid wearers in adjacent rooms — this is called overlap. This may be a problem in multi-screen cinemas or where confidentiality is required. In these cases infrared systems may be more suitable.
- Infrared systems work on different principles by converting a sound source into an infrared light signal and require special receiving headsets. This system is more suitable for controlled areas such as cinemas, theatres and lecture rooms where headsets can be borrowed from a central source. As the technology is based on light, sound cannot be picked up outside the room in which the infrared signals are generated.

Alarms and security

- Audible alarms should be supplemented by visual alarms for people with hearing impairments.
- Individual vibratory devices may be appropriate in some cases.
- Entryphones should contain an LED display to enable people with hearing impairments to use them.
- Security systems such as swipe cards and turnstiles should be detailed to allow use by people with sensory or mobility impairments.

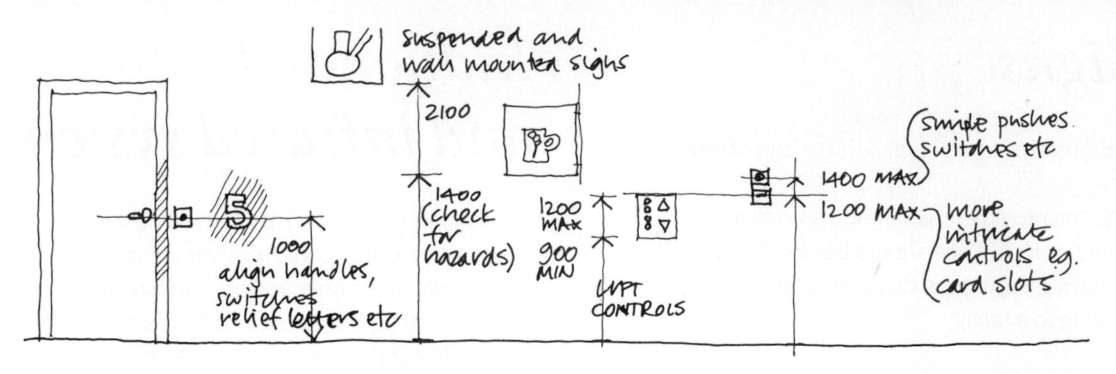

Controls

- Colour and tonal contrast should be used to ensure controls are distinguishable from their background.
- Controls that convey information (as in a lift for instance) should offer it in forms suitable for people with sensory impairments.

Surfaces

The selection of surfaces is of considerable importance to people with sight impairments, hearing impairments and mobility impairments. They can make the difference between a building that is easy and comfortable to use and one that is confusing or a struggle.

- Hard surfaces increase the amount of time for which sound reverberates which can confuse people with impaired hearing.
- Glossy floors and walls cause reflections which can mislead people with poor sight.
- For easy wheelchair passage floor surfaces should be non-directional, firmly-fixed and of shallow dense pile if carpeted.
- Junctions between different flooring materials should be carefully detailed so as not to provide an obstacle to wheelchair users or a tripping hazard for ambulant disabled people or people with poor sight.
- Distinguishability between surfaces and objects placed upon them such as walls and light switches or floors and litter bins achieved through a combination of colour, tonal and textural contrast helps people with impaired sight.
- Tonal contrast is as important as colour contrast as some sight conditions can confuse different colours of similar tone.
- Textured surfaces are important in providing information to people with little or no sight. Textured floors can warn of hazards or impart directional information; textured walls (of fine rather than rough grain) can alert people to the presence of facilities such as WCs or lifts where a key to the understanding of this system has been given beforehand.
- Wall coverings should not be busy or distracting for people with hearing impairments who have to concentrate when lip-reading a speaker standing against them.
- Floor surfaces should be slip-resistant. This is of particular importance to people who use walking aids such as sticks or crutches, and to older people.
- Floor areas that may become wet — just inside the entrance to covered shopping malls for example — should not become slippery.
- Bright boldly-patterned flooring should be avoided as it can create a confusing impression for people with impaired sight.

Lighting

Good lighting is essential for everyone to make the most of the information they receive via the eyes. People with sight impairments generally require greater levels of light than people with good sight — people over 60 need three times as much light as the average 20-year-old to achieve the same level of illumination — but some conditions make the eyes very sensitive to light.

- Lighting should be controllable and adjustable to meet the needs of the individual and the task they are working on.
- Passive infrared sensors can be used to detect dim light and activate booster lighting.
- Keeping windows, blinds and lamps clean maximises the amount of light available.
- Lighting can be used to accentuate texture and highlight colour thereby enhancing visual clues for people with sight impairments.
- Lights should be positioned where they do not cause glare, reflection, confusing shadows or pools of light and dark.
- Avoid positioning desks in front of windows where bright sunshine will cause the user's face to be in shadow and hence difficult to lip-read.
- Positioning lighting in unusual or unexpected places can create shadows and misleading visual effects.
- Uplighters placed above a standing person's eye level can deliver a comfortable, glare-free illumination.
- Fluorescent lights create a magnetic field which causes a hum in hearing aids. Lighting of this type should be specified with care where it cannot inconvenience people with hearing impairments.

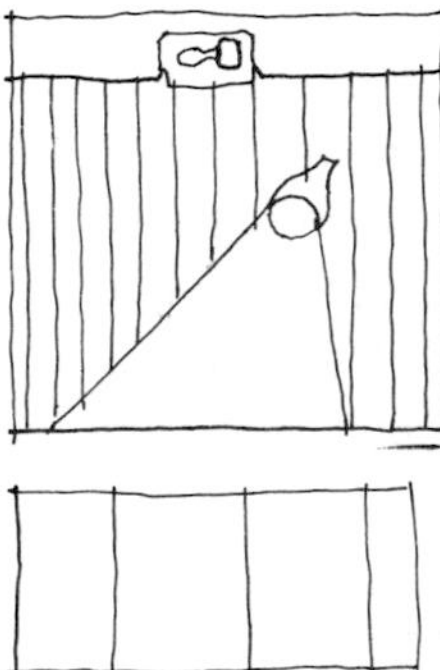

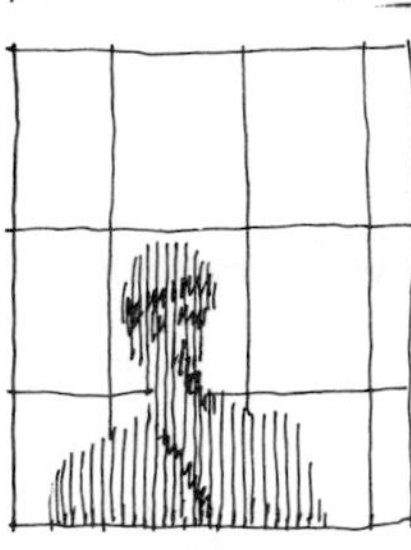

Services

- Heating units should be recessed wherever possible and exposed angles avoided.
- Supplementary heating units should be chosen with a view to minimising background noise which can be distracting and tiring for people with hearing impairments.
- Air conditioning units create a lot of background noise. They should be regularly maintained in order to reduce noise due to wear.
- The main power supply cable to a building generates a considerable magnetic field which can cause a loud hum in hearing aids. Care should be taken to route the cable away from public spaces.

Appendix one — *Building management*

Accessibility cannot be guaranteed by good design alone. How a building is managed in its day-to-day running will have a huge impact on how easy the building is to use by disabled people. For example, a spacious lift lobby with plenty of room for a wheelchair user to reverse into the lift is rendered useless if it is used for the temporary storage of boxes of stationery. The thoughtless addition of a new series of signs to direct people to a new facility can undermine a carefully chosen signage system thereby confusing people with poor sight or a learning disability. Installing an induction loop in a theatre or meeting room is pointless if the building management does not advertise its presence.

For these reasons it is important that those involved in making a building accessible, whether new or existing, contribute to the drafting of a building management manual. This can take the form of a simple loose-leaf binder with sections covering the following areas which explain the reasons behind the requirements:

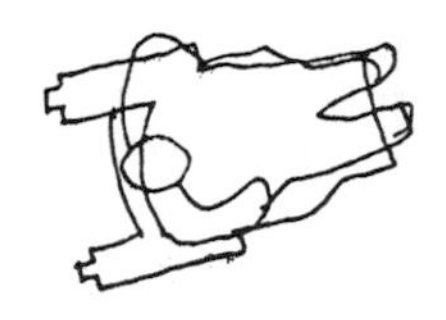

Car parking — ensuring that non-disabled drivers do not occupy bays intended for disabled people.

Routes — ensuring that external routes, ramps and steps are kept clean, unobstructed and, in winter, ice-free.

Doors — ensuring that door closers are regularly maintained, door ironmongery is kept clean and free moving, side-hung doors accompanying revolving doors are not kept locked.

Horizontal circulation — ensuring that spaces required for wheelchair manoeuvres are not obstructed by deliveries or storage.

Vertical circulation — ensuring that lifts are regularly checked to see that the lift car floor aligns with the structural floor, that short-rise lifts are not abused by people using them as goods lifts.

Lavatories — ensuring that supplies of toilet tissue and paper towels are regularly replenished and that the WC is not used as an unofficial storage area.

Signs — ensuring that new signs integrate with the existing signage, that signs are replaced correctly when removed for redecoration.

Maps — ensuring that maps of building interiors are updated when departments move offices within the building.

Induction loops and infrared systems — ensuring that installations are advertised and regularly checked.

Alarms and security — ensuring that alarm systems, including those in WCs, are regularly checked and that new staff are trained in alarm response procedures.

Surfaces — ensuring that cleaning and polishing does not render slip-resistant surfaces slippery. Ensuring that the junctions between different flooring materials do not become worn, presenting a tripping hazard. Ensuring that when flooring is renewed like is replaced by like. Ensuring that the redecoration of interiors does not compromise a carefully devised colour scheme designed to impart information to people with poor sight or impair contrast with features such as door frames, control panels, signs etc.

Lighting — ensuring that windows, lamps and blinds are kept clean in order to maximise available light. Ensuring that blown light bulbs are swiftly replaced.

There will, of course, be further sections relating specifically to the particular building and its functions and as access problems occur new sections should be added to the manual with guidance on how they can be prevented in future.

Appendix two — *Fire safety*

As Designing for Accessibility is intended as an introductory guide to the design of accessible buildings, it does not attempt to cover emergency egress from buildings in the same level of detail. It should be acknowledged, however, that this is a crucial subject area that should be considered at the same time as access.

The design of a building alone cannot ensure safety for the occupants in the case of a fire or other emergency. Means of escape strategies must be devised by the building's management in order to ensure safe, swift, orderly evacuation. Escape strategies for disabled building users will differ from those for able-bodied building users according to the amount of assistance they require in order to leave the building.

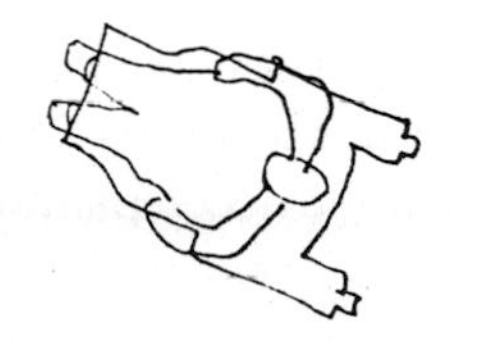

The Approved Document supporting Part B of the Building Regulations 1991 comprises the requirements for fire precautions in a building and guidance on meeting them. Detailed information on means of escape for disabled people is given in Part 8 of BS5588 *Fire Precautions in the Design, Construction and Use of Buildings.* This document considers the concepts of horizontal and vertical escape, proposing that disabled people evacuate themselves as far as possible horizontally to a fire-protected refuge space on or near the escape stairs. From there they can be evacuated vertically with the required assistance from the building management or fire brigade. BS5588 Part 8 states that lifts can be used to assist in the evacuation of disabled building users if they are encased within a fire-protected shaft and have their own independent electrical supply and control panel. Appendices give guidance on evacuation techniques.

The safe and competent evacuation of disabled employees depends in large part upon the creation of bespoke personal emergency egress plans (PEEPS) that take into account the difficulties the building presents, the requirements of the disabled person for assistance and the abilities of colleagues in giving assistance. Generic emergency evacuation plans can be devised to meet the needs of visitors. These will be fundamentally suited for the evacuation of wheelchair users or ambulant disabled people or people with sight impairments and will facilitate the safe evacuation of disabled visitors whose personal needs cannot be identified in advance.

Details of guidance concerning the creation of PEEPS and other documents about fire safety are given in appendix five.

Appendix three — *Legislation*

This appendix gives a summary of the main pieces of legislation and official guidance that relate to access for disabled people to buildings.

1970 The Chronically Sick and Disabled Persons Act
Section 4 requires that 'Any person undertaking the provision of any building or premises to which the public are admitted, whether on payment or otherwise, shall, in the means of access both to and within the building or premises, and in the parking facilities and sanitary conveniences to be available (if any), make provision, in so far as it is both reasonable and practicable, for the needs of members of the public visiting the building or premises who are disabled'.

Section 6 requires similar provision at places of accommodation, refreshment or entertainment, and section 8 relates to access and facilities at university and school buildings.

MHLG Circular 65/70
This document cites public halls, public libraries, theatres, cinemas and shops as 'obvious examples of buildings to which the public are to be admitted'. The circular confirms that 'provision' covers 'not only new construction but also the conversion of existing buildings'.

1976 The Chronically Sick and Disabled Persons (Amendment) Act
This extends the requirements of the 1970 Act to places of employment.

1979 BS5810 British Standard Code of Practice for Access for the Disabled to Buildings
This is a voluntary code of practice of guidance which sets down the essential provisions that need to be incorporated in buildings to ensure they can be conveniently used by disabled people. Currently under review.

1981 The Disabled Persons Act
The Act introduced sections to the Town and Country Planning Act 1971. Section 29a places a duty on the local planning authority when granting planning permission for any development covered by Section 4 of the CSDP Act 1970 to draw the attention of developers to the relevant provisions of the 1970 Act and to BS5810:1979. Section 29b makes similar provision in relation to educational buildings. Section 6 of the Act provided for the substitution of 'appropriate provision' for the wording 'provision, in so far as is in the circumstances both practicable and reasonable', of the 1970 Act. This section did not come into effect and its purpose is now superseded by Part M of the Building Regulations 1991.

Sections 29a and b of the 1971 Act have been replaced by Section 76 of the Town and Country Planning Act 1990.

1982 Department of the Environment (DoE) Circular 10/82
This suggests that developers be made aware of their obligations under the CSDP Act 1970 by means of a note accompanying the local planning authority's notice of the grant of planning permission. Local authorities are encouraged to designate one of their staff as

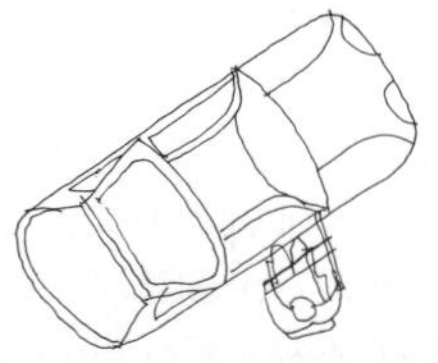

an 'access officer' to provide a clearly identified point of contact on questions of access for disabled people. The circular states that 'the arrangements for access to buildings can be a planning matter and the suitability of arrangements for use by the public, which includes disabled people, raises issues of public amenity which . . . can be material to a planning application . . . ,where appropriate, conditions may be attached to a grant of planning permission . . . '.

1984 Department of Education and Science (DES) Design Note 18 Access for Disabled People to Educational Buildings
The document covers access and facilities for disabled people in educational buildings. The requirements for access stated in Part M of the Building Regulations 1991 are satisfied by the relevant parts of Design Note 18.

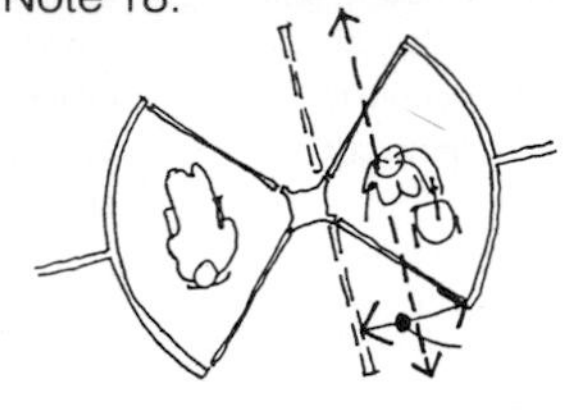

1988 BS5588:Part 8 British Standard Code of Practice for Means of Escape for Disabled People
Although not a statutory document it is cited in Part B of the Building Regulations 1991. It gives authoritative guidance on the design and management of buildings to enable the safe evacuation of people with disabilities in case of fire. The document includes guidance on the application of the code to existing buildings.

1992 The Building (Disabled People) Regulations: Part M Access for Disabled People
This was introduced on 1 June 1992 and supersedes the original Part M of the 1985 Building Regulations which was introduced on 14 December 1987. The revised Part M requires access and facilities for disabled people in all floors of new non-domestic buildings and applies in a limited way to some extensions.

The definition of disabled people now includes those with hearing or sight impairments as well as people who use wheelchairs or have difficulty walking.

The Approved Document supporting Part M gives technical guidance on the design of ramps, stairs, handrails, doors, lobbies, lifts, hotel bedrooms, sanitary accommodation, shower and changing cubicles and spectator seating. It also introduces, in certain circumstances, the use of wheelchair stairlifts or platform lifts and gives new guidance on levels of WC provision.

Appendix four — *Useful organisations and trade associations*

Centre for Accessible Environments
Nutmeg House
60 Gainsford Street,
London SE1 2NY

Tel: 0171-357 8182

The Centre is an information and training resource on accessibility for the construction industry, the care professions and disabled people. The Centre is committed to the provision of buildings and environments that are accessible to all users, including disabled and older people, and to the enhancement of quality in design. Services include technical information and advice, a journal *Access by Design*, a range of design guides and other material, access appraisals, a register of professionals with experience of designing for disabled people and an extensive seminar programme.

Access Committee for England
12 City Forum
250 City Road
London EC1V 8AF

Tel: 0171-250 0008
Minicom 0171-250 4119

The Access Committee, for which the Royal Association for Disability and Rehabilitation (RADAR) provides an administrative base, is a policy advisory committee whose objective is to promote the accessibility to disabled people of buildings and the built environment, including issues of housing.

The Guide Dogs for the Blind Association
Hillfields
Burghfield Common
Reading
Berkshire RG7 3YG

Tel: 01734 835555

The Association seeks to provide and train guide dogs, and support their owners. It can provide information to designers on features which guide dogs may require in a building.

Royal National Institute for the Blind
224 Great Portland Street
London W1N 6AA

Tel: 0171-388 1266

The RNIB aims to improve the quality of life for all people with a sight impairment. It operates a mobility unit which provides information on the needs of sight-impaired people to those responsible for shaping our built environment.

Partially Sighted Society
62 Salusbury Road
London NW6 6NS

Tel: 0171-372 1551

The Society aims to assist partially sighted people in their daily lives. It offers an environmental consultancy service for building designers seeking to meet the needs of people with sight impairments.

Royal National Institute for Deaf People
105 Gower Street
London WC1E 6AH

Tel: 0171-387 8033

The RNID works to improve the quality of life for deaf and hard of hearing people in the United Kingdom. It provides information on induction loops, infrared hearing enhancement systems and other measures that meet the needs of people with hearing impairments.

Hearing Concern
7-11 Armstrong Road
London W3 7JL

Tel: 0181-743 1110

Hearing Concern (previously known as the British Association of the Hard of Hearing) acts as an information and advice centre for problems concerning people with impaired hearing. It can assist designers with the installation and testing of hearing enhancement systems in buildings.

National Deaf Children's Society
Technology Information Centre
4 Church Road
Birmingham B15 3TD

Tel: 0121-454 5151

The Society's Technical Information Centre has a wide variety of environmental aids on display including induction loops, infrared systems, smoke alarms, and doorbell and telephone indicators.

Disabled Living Foundation
380-384 Harrow Road
London W9 2HU

Tel: 0171-289 6111

The DLF offers an information service on aids and equipment that help people with disabilities in their daily lives. It administers a comprehensive database of manufacturers many of whose products can be used by disabled people in public and employment buildings.

Readers seeking information on particular building products suitable for use by everyone, including elderly and disabled people, may find the following trade associations helpful. Most offer an information service on their members' product ranges.

Floor surfaces
British Floorcovering Manufacturers Association
10 Bristol Road
Kemptown
Brighton BN2 1AP

Tel: 01273 694285

British Rubber Manufacturers Association
90 Tottenham Court Road
London W1P 0BR

Tel: 0171-580 2794

Textured paving
Interpave (The Concrete Block Paving Association)
60 Charles Street
Leicester LE1 1FB

Tel: 01533 536161

Signs
British Sign Association
Swan House
207 Balham High Road
London SW17 7BQ

Tel: 0181-675 7241

Doors and door ironmongery
Automatic Door Suppliers Association
411 Limpsfield Road
The Green
Warlingham
Surrey CR6 9HA

Tel: 01883 624961

Guild of Architectural Ironmongers
8 Stepney Green
London E1 3JU

Tel: 0171-790 3431

Association of Builders' Hardware Manufacturers
Heath Street
Tamworth
Staffs B79 7JH

Tel: 01827 52337

Lift equipment
National Association of Lift Makers
33-34 Devonshire Street
London W1N 1RF

Tel: 0171-935 3013

Sanitary equipment
Disabled Living Foundation
380-384 Harrow Road
London W9 2HU

Tel: 0171-289 6111

British Bathroom Council
Federation House
Station Road
Stoke on Trent ST4 2RT

Tel: 01782 747074

Outdoor seating
Institute of Leisure and Amenity Management
ILAM House
Lower Basildon
Reading RG8 9NE

Tel: 01491 874222

Association of Play Industries
23 Brighton Road
South Croydon CR2 6EA

Tel: 0181-681 1242

Appendix five — *Further reading*

Part M Design Sheets, *by Stephen Thorpe BArch RIBA, Centre for Accessible Environments 1990*
Detailed design guidance covering approaches and entrances, internal spaces, restaurants, en suite hotel bathrooms and shops.

Sports and Leisure Facilities Design Sheets, *by Stephen Thorpe BArch RIBA, Centre for Accessible Environments 1991*
Detailed guidance on the design of swimming pools, audience and spectator seating, countryside recreation and nature trails, shower and changing cubicles.

Good Loo Design Guide, *by Stephen Thorpe BArch RIBA, Centre for Accessible Environments 1988*
Photographs and text explain how disabled people actually use a loo; annotated drawings give information on layout and equipment.

Part M Planner, *by Michael Burrows RIBA, Centre for Accessible Environments 1991*
A poster-format check-list with sketches showing the basic dimensions and features necessary to meet the requirements of Part M.

Wheelchair Template, *by Stephen Thorpe BArch RIBA, Centre for Accessible Environments 1991*
An A5 plastic template comprising cutouts of a standard wheelchair at scales 1:20 and 1:50, a recommended WC layout at 1:50 and an anthropometric drawing showing average reach heights from a wheelchair at 1:20.

Tourism for All: Providing Accessible Accommodation, *by John Penton MBE RIBA, Holiday Care Service/English Tourist Board 1990*

Part M: Access and Facilities for Disabled People, *Approved Document 1992 edition Department of the Environment, HMSO 1991*

BS5810:1979 Code of Practice for Access for the Disabled to Buildings, *BSI*

BS5588: Part 8:1988 Fire Precautions in the Design, Construction and Use of Buildings — Code of Practice for Means of Escape for Disabled People, *BSI*

PD6523:1989 Information on Access to and Movement Within and Around Buildings and on Certain Facilities for Disabled People, *BSI*

Fire Safety at Work, Home Office/Scottish Home and Health Department, *HMSO 1989*

Fire Safety Management in Hotels and Boarding Houses, *Home Office/The Scottish Office, HMSO 1991*

Guide to Fire Precautions in Existing Places of Entertainment and Like Premises, *Home Office/Scottish Home and Health Department, HMSO 1990*

Personal Emergency Egress Plans, *Northern Officer Group, c/o Equal Opportunities Department Wakefield MDC, 1993, available from Centre for Accessible Environments*

Design Insights, *by Rod Wilson and Peter Barker, RNIB due to be published 1995*

Lighting and Low Vision, *Partially Sighted Society and the Electricity Association 1988*

Providing for People with Impaired Vision: Access Guide, *Partially Sighted Society 1990*

Induction Loops in Public Places, *leaflet from RNID*

Aids to Daily Living, *leaflet from RNID*

Informal Countryside Recreation for Disabled People, *Countryside Commission 1994*

Reducing Mobility Handicaps – Towards a Barrier Free Environment, *The Institution of Highways and Transportation 1991*

The Use of Dropped Kerbs and Tactile Surfaces at Pedestrian Crossing Points, *Dept of Transport Disability Unit Circular 1/91, 1992*

Index

CENTRE FOR *Accessible* ENVIRONMENTS

The Centre is an information and training resource on accessibility for the construction industry, the care professions and disabled people. The Centre is committed to the provision of buildings and environments that are accessible to all users, including disabled and older people, and to the enhancement of quality in design. It is concerned to ensure that users have access not only to buildings but to the full range of services that buildings provide. The Centre believes that buildings that are fully accessible to people with sensory as well as mobility disabilities are more convenient, safer and hospitable to all.

Services include:

- technical information and advice by telephone and letter
- advice on compliance with Part M of the Building Regulations
- access appraisals — assessment of access provision in architects' drawings
- a comprehensive training programme on topics of current concern to the construction industry and care professions
- the journal *Access by Design* published three times a year
- Design guides, specifiers' handbooks, and other publications
- a register of member professionals with experience of designing for people with disabilities

For more information about the Centre's services and to find out how to join, please write or telephone.

CENTRE FOR *Accessible* ENVIRONMENTS

Nutmeg House,
60 Gainsford Street, London SE1 2NY.
Tel: 0171-357 8182